The Science of Living

Alfred Adler

The Science of Living

The present edition is a reproduction of previous publication of this classic work. Minor typographical errors may have been corrected without note; however, for an authentic reading experience the spelling, punctuation, and capitalization have been retained from the original text.

ISBN: 979-8-88830-216-3

CONTENTS

CONTENTS

A NOTE ON THE AUTHOR AND HIS WORK

DR. ALFRED ADLER'S work in psychology, while it is scientific and general in method, is essentially the study of the separate personalities we are, and is therefore called Individual Psychology. Concrete, particular, unique human beings are the subjects of this psychology, and it can only be truly learned from the men, women and children we meet.

The supreme importance of this contribution to modern psychology is due to the manner in which it reveals how all the activities of the soul are drawn together into the service of the individual, how all his faculties and strivings are related to one end. We are enabled by this to enter into the ideals, the difficulties, the efforts and discouragements of our fellow-men, in such a way that we may obtain a whole and living picture of each as a personality. In this co-ordinating idea, something like finality is achieved, though we must understand it as finality of foundation. There has never before been a method so rigorous and yet adaptable for following the fluctuations of that most fluid, variable and elusive of all realities, the individual human soul.

Since Adler regards not only science but even intelligence itself as the result of the communal efforts of humanity, we shall find his consciousness of his own unique contribution more than usually tempered by recognition of his collaborators, both past and contemporary. It will therefore be useful to consider Adler's relation to the movement called Psycho-analysis, and first of all to recall, however briefly, the philosophic impulses which inspired the psycho-analytic movement as a whole.

The conception of the Unconscious as vital memory biological memory is common to modern psychology as a whole. But Freud, from the first a specialist in hysteria, took the memories of success or failure in the sexual life, as of the first and almost the only importance. Jung, a psychiatrist of genius, has tried to widen this

1

distressingly narrow view, by seeking to reveal the super-individual or racial memories which, he believes, have as much power as the sexual and a higher kind of value for life.

It was left to Alfred Adler, a physician of wide and general experience, to unite the conception of the Unconscious more firmly with biological reality. A man of the original school of psycho-analysts, he had done much work by that method of analyzing memories out of their coagulated emotional state into clearness and objectivity. But he showed that the whole scheme of memory is different in every individual. Individuals do not form their unconscious memories all around the same central motive not all around sexuality, for instance. In every individual we find an individual way of selecting its experiences from all possible experience. What is the principle of that selectivity? Adler has answered that it is, fundamentally, the organic consciousness of a need, of some specific inferiority which has to be compensated. It is as though every soul had consciousness of its whole physical reality, and were concentrated, with sleepless insistence, upon achieving compensation for the defects in it.

Thus the whole life of the small man, for instance, would be interpretable as a struggle to achieve immediate greatness in some way, and that of a deaf man to obtain a compensation for not hearing. It is not so simple as that, of course, for a system of defects may give rise to a constellation of guiding ideas, and also in human life we have to deal with imaginary inferiorities and fantastic strivings, but even here the principle is the same.

The sexual life, far from controlling all activities, fits perfectly into the frame of those more important strivings, for it is pre-eminently under the control of emotion, and emotion is moulded by the entire vital history. Thus a Freudian analysis gives a true account of the sexual consequences of a given life-line, but it is a true diagnosis only in that sense.

Psychology becomes now for the first time rooted in biology. The tendencies of the soul, and the mind's development, are seen to be

2

controlled from the first by the effort to compensate for organic defects or for positions of inferiority. Everything that is exceptional or individual in the disposition of an organic being originates in this way. The principle is common to man and animal, probably even to the vegetable kingdom also; and the special endowments of species are to be taken as arising from experience of defects and inferiorities in relation to their environment, which has been successfully compensated by activity, growth and structure.

There is nothing new in the idea of compensation as a biological principle, for it has been long known that the body will over-develop certain parts in compensation for the injury of others. If one kidney ceases to function, for instance, the other develops abnormally until it does the work of both; if the heart springs a leak in a valve, the whole organ grows larger to allow for its loss of efficiency, and when nervous tissue is destroyed, adjacent tissue of another kind endeavours to take on the nerve-function. The compensatory developments of the whole organism to meet the exigencies of any special work or exertion are too numerous and well known to need illustration. But it is Dr. Adler who has first transferred this principle bodily to psychology as a fundamental idea, and demonstrated the part it plays in the soul and intellect.

Adler recommends the study of Individual Psychology not only to doctors, but generally to laymen and especially to teachers. Culture in psychology has become a general necessity, and must be firmly advocated in the teeth of popular opposition to it, which is founded upon the notion that modern psychology requires an unhealthy concentration of the mind upon cases of disease and misery. It is true that the literature of psychoanalysis has revealed the most central and the most universal evils in modern society. But it is not now a question of contemplating our errors, it is necessary that we should learn by them. We have been trying to live as though the soul of man were not a reality, as though we could build up a civilized life in defiance of psychic truths. What Adler proposes is not the universal study of psycho-pathology, but the practical reform of society and culture in accordance with a positive and

3

scientific psychology to which he has contributed the first principles. But this is impossible if we are too much afraid of the truth. The clearer consciousness of right aims in life, which is indispensable to us, cannot be gained without a deeper understanding also of the mistakes in which we are involved. We may not desire to know ugly facts, but the more truly we are aware of life, the more clearly we perceive the real errors which frustrate it, much as the concentration of a light gives definition to the shadows.

A positive psychology, useful for human life, cannot be derived from the psychic phenomena alone, still less from pathological manifestations. It requires also a regulative principle, and Adler has not shrunk from this necessity, by recognizing, as if it were of absolute metaphysical validity, the logic of our communal life in the world.

Recognizing this principle, we must proceed to estimate the psychology of the individual in relation to it. The way in which an individual's inner life is related to the communal being is distinguishable in three "life-attitudes," as they are called his general reactions to society, to work and to love.

By their feeling towards society as a whole to any other and to all others man and woman may know how much social courage they possess. The feeling of inferiority is always manifested in a sense of fear or uncertainty in the presence of society, whether its outward expression is one of timidity or defiance, reserve or over-anxiety. All feelings of innate suspicion or hostility, of an undefined caution and desire for some concealment, when such feelings affect the individual in social relations generally, evince the same tendency to withdraw from reality, which inhibits self-affirmation. The ideal, or rather normal, attitude to society is an unstrained and unconsidered assumption of human equality unchanged by any inequalities of position. Social courage depends upon this feeling of secure membership of the human family, a feeling which depends upon the harmony of one's own life. By the tone of his feeling towards his

4

neighbours, his township and nation and to other nationalities, and even by his reactions when he reads of all these things in his newspaper, a man may infer how securely his own soul is grounded in itself.

The attitude towards work is closely dependent upon this self-security in society. In the occupation by which a man earns his share in social goods and privileges, he has to face the logic of social needs. If he has too great a sense of weakness or division from society, it will make him unable to believe that his worth will ever be recognized, and he will not even work for recognition: instead, he will play for safety, and work for money or advantage only, suppressing his own valuation of what is the truest service he can render. He will always be afraid to supply or demand the best, for fear it may not pay. Or he may be always seeking for some quiet backwater of the economic life, where he can do something just as he likes himself, without proper consideration of either usefulness or profit. In both cases it is not only society that suffers by not getting the best service: the individual who has not attained his proper social significance is also deeply dissatisfied. The modern world is full of men, both successful and unsuccessful in a worldly sense, who are in open conflict with their occupation. They do not believe in it, and they blame social and economic conditions with some real justice; but it is also a fact that they have often had too little courage to fight for the best value in their economic function. They were afraid to claim the right to give what they genuinely believed in, or else they felt disdainful of the service society really needed of them. Hence they pursued their gain in an individualistic or even furtive spirit. We must, of course, recognize that so much is wrong in the organization of society, that, besides the possibility of making mistakes of judgment, the individual who is determined to render real social service has often to face heavy opposition. But it is precisely that sense of struggle to give his best which the individual needs no less than society benefits by it. One cannot love a vocation which does not afford some experience of victory over difficulties, and not merely of compromise with them.

5

It is the third of these life-attitudes the attitude to love which determines the course of the erotic life. Where the two previous life-attitudes, to society and to work, have been rightly adjusted, this last comes right by itself. Where it is distorted and wrong it cannot be improved by itself apart from the others. Although we can think how to improve the social relations and the occupation, a concentration of thought upon the individual sex-problem is almost sure to make it worse. For this is far more the sphere of results than of causes. A soul that is defeated in ordinary social life, or thwarted in its occupation, acts in the sex-life as though it were trying to obtain compensation for the kinds of expression of which it fails in their proper spheres. This is actually the best way in which we can understand all sexual vagaries, whether they isolate the individual, degrade the sexual partner or in any way distort the instinct. The friendships of an individual also are integral with the love-life as a whole; not, as the first psycho-analysts imagined, because friendship is a sublimation of sexual attraction, but the other way about. Sexual compulsion sex as an insubordinate psychic factor is an abnormal substitute for the vitalizing intimacy of useful friendships, and homosexuality is always the consequence of incapability for love.

The meaning and value which we give to sensations are also united closely with the erotic life, as many good poets have testified. The quality of our feeling for Nature, our response to the beauty of sea and land, and to significances of form and sound and colour, as well as our confidence in scenes of storm and gloom, are all involved with our integrity as lovers. The aesthetic life, with all it means to art and culture, is thus ultimately derived, through individuals, from social courage and intelligent usefulness.

We ought not to regard the communal feeling as something to be created with difficulty. It is as natural and inherent as egoism itself, and indeed as a principle of life it has priority. We have not to create, but only to liberate, it where it is repressed. It is the saving principle of life as we experience it. If anyone thinks that the services of 'busmen railwaymen and milkmen would be rendered as well as they are without the presence of very much instinctive communal feeling he must be suspected of a highly neurotic scheme of apperception. What inhibits it is, to speak bluntly, the enormous vanity of the human soul, which is, moreover, so subtle that no professional psychologist before Adler had been able to demonstrate it, though a few artists had divined its omnipresence. All unsuspected as it often is, the ambition of many a minor journalist or shop-assistant, to say nothing of the great ones of the world, would be enough to bring about the fall of an archangel. Every feeling of inferiority that has embittered his contact with life has fed the imagination of greatness with another god-like assumption until, in many cases, the fantasy has become so inflated as to demand not even supremacy in this world for its appeasement, but the creation of a new world altogether, and to be the god of it. This revelation of the depth of human nature is verified, not so strikingly from the study of cases of practical ambition, however Napoleonic, as from those of passive resistance, procrastination, and malingering, for it is these which show most clearly that an individual who feels painfully unable to dominate the real world will refuse to co-operate with it, at whatever disadvantage to himself, partly in order to tyrannize over a narrower sphere, and partly even from an irrational feeling that the real world, without his divine assistance, will some day crumble and shrink to his own diminished measure.[1]

The question is thus raised, how should we act, knowing this tendency to inordinate vanity in the human soul, and that we dare not merely add to that vanity by assuming ourselves to be miraculous exceptions? Adler's reply is that we should preserve a certain attitude to all our experience, which he calls the attitude of "half-and-half." Our conception of normal behaviour should be to

---

[1] In case this should seem an exaggeration, we may recall the fact that nearly all the narrowest kind of sects, religious or secular, have a belief in world-catastrophe: the world from which! they have withdrawn, and which they despair of converting, is to be brought to destruction, and only a remnant will survive, who will be of their own persuasion.

allow the world or society, or the person with whom we are confronted, to be somehow in the right equally with ourselves. We should not depreciate either ourselves or our environment; but, assuming that each is one-half in the right, affirm the reality of ourselves and others equally. This applies not only to contacts with other souls, but to our mental reactions towards rainy weather, holidays or comforts that we cannot afford, and even to the omnibus we have just missed.

Rightly understood, this is not an ideal of difficult and distasteful humility. It is in reality a tremendous assumption of worth, to claim exactly equal reality and omnipotence with the whole of the rest of creation, in whatever particular manifestation we may be meeting with it. To claim less than this is a false humility, for what results from any contact we make does in fact depend for half its reality upon the way in which we make it. The individual should affirm his part in everything which occurs to him, as his own half of it.

This is often a particularly difficult counsel to keep in relation to the occupation. In their business, people face more naked realities than are usually allowed to appear in social life; and it is often almost impossible to allow equal validity to one's own aims and to the conditions of a disorganized world. To do so, means the admission that conditions, just such as they are, are one's real problem and, indeed, one's proper sphere of action. The division of labour, logical and useful as it is in itself, has given opportunity for human megalomania to create entirely false inequalities, distinctions and injustices, so that we live in an economic disorder which will hardly hold together. To such crazy conditions, the best of men often find it difficult to oppose themselves with perseverance, equally granting its reality and working for its reform. They are tempted to acquiesce in disorder by some inner subterfuge, or to devote themselves to superficial remedies which evade the real problem; and sometimes they treat their work-life as an unavoidable contamination by things inherently squalid, quite unaware that such an attitude makes them conceited, haughty and, in a profound sense, unscrupulous. It occurs to very few that the right way would be to make alliance on human grounds with others in the same predicament and profession, to assert its proper dignity as a social service and improve it; but this is the only way in which the individual can really be reconciled with his economic function. Many of those who complain most about the conditions prevailing in their work are doing nothing whatever to reorganize it as a function of human life, and never think of attacking the anarchic individualism which is its ruin. We derive it from Individual Psychology, as a categorical imperative, that every man's duty is to work to make his profession, whatever it may be, into a brotherhood, a friendship, a social unity with a powerful morale of co-operation, and that if a man does not want to do this his own psychological state is precarious. It is true that now, in many professions, the task that this presents is terribly difficult. It is all the more essential that the effort should be made towards integration. For a man's work will never liberate the forces of his psyche unless he is striving, in a large sense, to make it the expression of his whole being, and his idea of his profession must be not only an executive in which he has independence of action, but also a legislative in which he has some authority of direction. In a man's business life the half-and-half valuation leads equally to recognition of reality and to struggle with it by the only realistic method, which is necessarily co-operative.

The pedagogic principles of Individual Psychology, infallible as far as they go, are useless without this practical work of social organization. What has been written above of an individual's duty in his occupation applies in a large sense to his entire social function. A person's function includes active membership of his nation and of humanity, to say nothing of his family. There is a certain parliament which rises for no vacation, and to whose decisions all elected assemblies must in the end defer. It meets in schools, markets, and everywhere on sea and land, for it is the Parliament of Man, in which every word or look exchanged, whether of courtesy or recrimination, of wisdom or folly, has its measure of importance in the affairs of the race. It is everyone's interest to make this wide assembly more united and its discussion

9

more intelligible, for none of us has any real human existence except by reflection from it. When its conclaves are peaceful, all our lives are heightened in tone, health and wealth accrues and arts and education flourish; when its conversation is reserved and suspicious, work fails, men starve and children languish. In the heat of its dissensions we perish by the million. All its decrees, by which we live or die, and grow or decay, are rooted in our individual attitudes towards man, woman and child in every relation of life.

When we face, objectively, this fact of the relation of all souls and their mutual responsibility, what are we to think of the inner confusion of the neurotic? Is it not simply a narrowing of the sphere of interest, an over-concentration upon certain personal or subjective gains? The neurotic soul is the result of treating the rest of humanity as though its life and aims were altogether of less importance than one's own, and thus losing interest in any larger life. Paradoxically, it often happens that a neurotic has very large schemes of saving himself and others. He is intelligent enough to try to compensate his real sense of isolation and impotence in the human assembly, by a fantasy of exaggerated importance and beneficent activity. He may want to reform education, to abolish war, to establish universal brotherhood or create a new culture, and even plans or joins societies with these aims. He is defeated in such aims, of course, by the unreality of his contact with others and with life as a whole. It is as though he had taken a standpoint outside of life altogether and were trying to direct it by some unexplained magic.

Modern city life especially, with its intellectualism, gives unlimited scope for the neurotic thus to compensate his real unsociability with imaginary messianism, and the result is the disintegration of a people full of saviours who are not on speaking terms.

What is needed, of course, is something very different. It is not that the individual should renounce messianism; for it is a fact that a share of responsibility for the whole future of the race is his alone. It is only necessary that he should take a reasonable view of his power to save society, correctly viewed from his own standpoint:

10

he must become able to regard his immediate personal relations and his occupations as if they were of world-importance, for in fact they are so, being the only world-meaning an individual has. When they are chaotic or wrong, it is because we do not, in day-to-day experience, treat them as things of universal meaning. We sometimes treat them as important, no doubt, but generally in a personal sense only.

This tendency of the modern soul, to narrow the sphere of interest, both practically and ideally, is most difficult to subdue, because it is reinforced by the scheme of apperception. For that reason an individual alone cannot do it, excepting only in rare cases. He needs conference with other minds, and an entirely new kind of conference. A resolution to treat one's immediate surroundings and daily activities as if they were the supreme significance of life brings an individual immediately into conflict with internal resistances of his own, and often with external difficulties also, which he cannot at once understand and which no others could rightly estimate unless they were making the same experiment. Hence, the practice of Individual Psychology demands that its students should submit themselves to mutual scrutiny, each one to be estimated by the others as a whole personality. This practice, striking at the root of the false individualism which is the basis of all neurosis, is naturally very difficult to initiate. Upon its success, however, depends the whole future of psycho-analysis as an influence in life at large, outside of clinics and consulting rooms.

In Vienna the work of such groups has already made itself felt in education. The co-operation it has established between teachers and medical practitioners has revolutionized the work of certain schools, and established an equality between teachers and pupils and between pupils themselves, which has cured many children of criminal tendencies, dullness and laziness. Abolition of competition and the cultivation of encouragement have been found to liberate the energy of both pupils and teachers. These changes are already affecting the surrounding family life, which comes into question immediately the child is psychologically considered. Education, though naturally the first, is not the only sphere of life which ought to be invaded by the activity of such groups. Business and political circles, which experience the deadlock of modern life most acutely, need to be vitalized with knowledge of human nature, which they have forgotten how to recognize.

It is for this work of releasing a new energy for daily life and *its reformation, that Alfred Adler has founded the International Society for Individual Psychology. The culture of human behaviour which this work has begun already to propagate might well be mistaken for an almost platitudinous ethics, but for two things its practical results, and the background of scientific method out of which it is appearing. In his realistic grasp of the social nature of the individual's problem and his inexorable demonstration of the unity of health and harmonious behaviour, Adler resembles no one so much as the great Chinese thinkers. If the occidental world is not too far gone to make use of his service, he may well come to be known as the Confucius of the West.

PHILLIPE MAIRET

12

CHAPTER ONE

THE SCIENCE OF LIVING

ONLY a science which is directly related to life, said the great philosopher William James, is really a science. It might also be said that in a science which is directly related to life theory and practice become almost inseparable. The science of life, precisely because it models itself directly on the movement of life, becomes a science of living. These considerations apply with special force to the science of Individual Psychology. Individual Psychology tries to see individual lives as a whole and regards each single reaction, each movement and impulse as an articulated part of an individual attitude towards life. Such a science is of necessity oriented in a practical sense, for with the aid of knowledge we can correct and alter our attitudes. Individual Psychology is thus prophetic in a double sense: not only does it predict what will happen, but, like the prophet Jonah, it predicts what will happen in order that it should not happen.

The science of Individual Psychology developed out of the effort to understand that mysterious creative power of life that power which expresses itself in the desire to develop, to strive and to acheive and even to compensate for defeats in one direction by striving for success in another. This power is ideological it expresses itself in the striving after a goal, and in this striving every bodily and psychic movement is made to co-operate. It is thus absurd to study bodily movements and mental conditions abstractly without relation to an individual whole. It is absurd, for instance, that in criminal psychology we should pay so much more attention to the crime than to the criminal. It is the criminal, not the crime that counts, and no matter how much we contemplate the criminal act we shall never understand its criminality unless we see it as an episode in the life of a particular individual. The same outward act may be criminal in one case and not criminal in another. The important thing is to understand the individual context the goal of an individual's life which marks the line of direction for all his acts and movements. This goal enables us to understand the hidden meaning behind the various separate acts we see them as parts of a whole. Vice versa when we study the parts provided we study them as parts of a whole we get a better sense of the whole.

In the author's own case the interest in psychology developed out of the practice of medicine. The practice of medicine provided the teleological or purposive viewpoint which is necessary for the understanding of psychological facts. In medicine we see all organs striving to develop towards definite goals. They have definite forms which they achieve upon maturity. Moreover, in cases where there are organic defects we always find nature making special efforts to overcome the deficiency, or else to compensate for it by developing another organ to take over the functions of the defective one. Life always seeks to continue, and the life force never yields to external obstacles without a struggle.

Now the movement of the psyche is analogous to the movement of organic life. In each mind there is the conception of a goal or ideal to get beyond the present state, and to overcome the present deficiencies and difficulties by postulating a concrete aim for the future. By means of this concrete aim or goal the individual can think and feel himself superior to the difficulties of the present because he has in mind his success of the future. Without the sense of a goal individual activity would cease to have any meaning. All evidence points to the fact that the fixing of this goal giving it a concrete form must take place early in life, during the formative period of childhood. A kind of prototype or model of a matured personality begins to develop at this time. We can imagine how the process takes place. A child, being weak, feels inferior and finds itself in a situation which it cannot bear. Hence it strives to develop, and it strives to develop along a line of direction fixed by the goal which it chooses for itself. The material used for development at this stage is less important than the goal which decides the line of direction. How this goal is fixed it is difficult to say, but it is

14

obvious that such a goal exists and that it dominates the child's every movement. Little is indeed understood about powers, impulses, reasons, abilities or disabilities at this early period. As yet there is really no key, for the direction is definitely established only after the child has fixed its goal. Only when we see the direction in which a life is tending can we guess what steps will be taken in the future.

When the prototype that early personality which embodies the goal is formed, the line of direction is established and the individual becomes definitely oriented. It is this fact which enables us to predict what will happen later in life. The individual's apperceptions are from then on bound to fall into a groove established by the line of direction. The child will not perceive given situations as they actually exist, but according to a personal scheme of apperception that is to say, he will perceive situations under the prejudice of his own interests.

An interesting fact that has been discovered in this connection is that children with organic defects connect all their experiences with the function of the defective organ. For instance, a child having stomach trouble shows an abnormal interest in eating, while one with defective eyesight is more preoccupied with things visible. This preoccupation is in keeping with the private scheme of apperception which we have said characterizes all persons. It might be suggested, therefore, that in order to find out where a child's interest lies we need only to ascertain which organ is defective. But things do not work out quite so simply. The child does not experience the fact of organ inferiority in the way that an external observer sees it, but as modified by its own scheme of apperception. Hence while the fact of organ inferiority counts as an element in the child's scheme of apperception, the external observation of the inferiority does not necessarily give the cue to the scheme of apperception.

The child is steeped in a scheme of relativity, and in this he is indeed like the rest of us none of us is blessed with the knowledge of the absolute truth. Even our science is not blessed with absolute

15

truth. It is based on common sense, which is to say that it is ever changing and that it is content gradually to replace big mistakes by smaller ones. We all make mistakes, but the important thing is that we can correct them.

Such correction is easier at the time of the formation of the prototype. And when we do not correct them at that time, we may correct the mistakes later on by recalling the whole situation of that period. Thus if we are confronted with the task of treating a neurotic patient, our problem is to discover, not the ordinary mistakes he makes in later life, but the very fundamental mistakes made early in his life in the course of the constitution of his prototype. If we discover these mistakes, it is possible to correct them by appropriate treatment.

In the light of Individual Psychology the problem of inheritance thus decreases in importance. It is not what one has inherited that is important, but what one does with his inheritance in the early years that is to say, the prototype that is built up in the childhood environment. Heredity is of course responsible for inherited organic defects, but our problem there is simply to relieve the particular difficulty and place the child in a favorable situation. As a matter of fact we have even a great advantage here, inasmuch as when we see the defect we know how to act accordingly. Oftentimes a healthy child without any inherited defects may fare worse through malnutrition or through any of the many errors in upbringing.

In the case of children born with imperfect organs it is the psychological situation which is all-important. Because these children are placed in a more difficult situation they show marked indications of an exaggerated feeling of inferiority. At the time the prototype is being formed they are already more interested in themselves than in others, and they tend to continue that way later on in life. Organic inferiority is not the only cause of mistakes in the prototype: other situations may also cause the same mistakes the situations of pampered and hated children, for instance. We shall have occasion later on to describe these situations more in detail

16

and to present actual case histories illustrating the three situations which are particularly unfavorable, that of children with imperfect organs, that of petted children, and that of hated children. For the present it is sufficient to note that these children grow up handicapped and that they constantly fear attacks inasmuch as they have grown up in an environment in which they never learned independence.

It is necessary to understand the social interest from the very outset since it is the most important part of our education, of our treatment and of our cure. Only such persons as are courageous, self-confident and at home in the world can benefit both by the difficulties and by the advantages of life. They are never afraid. They know that there are difficulties, but they also know that they can overcome them. They are prepared for all the problems of life, which are invariably social problems. From a human standpoint it is necessary to be prepared for social behavior. The three types of children we have mentioned develop a prototype with a lesser degree of social interest. They have not the mental attitude which is conducive to the accomplishment of what is necessary in life or to the solution of its difficulties. Feeling defeated, the prototype has a mistaken attitude towards the problems of life and tends to develop the personality on the useless side of life. On the other hand our task in treating such patients is to develop behavior on the useful side and to establish in general a useful attitude towards life and society.

Lack of social interest is equivalent to being oriented towards the useless side of life. The individuals who lack social interest are those who make up the groups of problem children, criminals, insane persons, and drunkards. Our problem in their case is to find means to influence them to go back to the useful side of life and to make them interested in others. In this way it may be said that our so-called Individual Psychology is actually a social psychology.

After the social interest, our next task is to find out the difficulties that confront the individual in his development. This task is

17

somewhat more confusing at first glance, but it is in reality not very complicated. We know that every petted child becomes a hated child. Our civilization is such that neither society nor the family wishes to continue the pampering process indefinitely. A pampered child is very soon confronted with life's problems. In school he finds himself in a new social institution, with a new social problem. He does not want to write or play with his fellows, for his experience has not prepared him for the communal life of the school. In fact his experiences as lived through at the prototype stage make him afraid of such situations and make him look for more pampering. Now the characteristics of such an individual are not inherited far from it for we can deduce them from a knowledge of the nature of his prototype and his goal. Because he has the particular characteristics conducive to his moving in the direction of his goal, it is not possible for him to have characteristics that would tend in any other direction.

The next step in the science of living lies in the study of the feelings. Not only does the axis line, the line of direction posited by the goal, affect individual characteristics, physical movements, expressions and general outward symptoms, but it dominates the life of the feelings as well. It is a remarkable thing that individuals always try to justify their attitudes by feelings. Thus if a man wants to do good work, we will find this idea magnified and dominating his whole emotional life. We can conclude that the feelings always agree with the individual's viewpoint of his task: they strengthen the individual in his bent for activity. We always do that which we would do even without the feelings, and the feelings are simply an accompaniment to our acts.

We can see this fact quite clearly in dreams, the discovery of whose purpose was perhaps one of the latest achievements of Individual Psychology. Every dream has of course a purpose, although this was never clearly understood until now. The purpose of a dream expressed in general and not specific terms is to create a certain movement of feeling or emotion, which movement of emotion in turn furthers the movement of the dream. It is an interesting commentary on the old idea that a dream is always a deception. We dream in the way that we would like to behave. Dreams are an emotional rehearsal of plans and attitudes for waking behavior a rehearsal, however, in which the actual play may never come off. In this sense dreams are deceptive the emotional imagination gives us the thrill of action without the action.

This characteristic of dreams is also found in our waking life. We always have a strong inclination to deceive ourselves emotionally we always want to persuade ourselves to go the way of our prototypes as they were formed in the fourth or fifth year of life.

The analysis of the prototype is next in order in our scheme of science. As we have said, at four or five the prototype is already built up, and so we have to look for impressions made on the child before or at that time. These impressions can be quite varied, far more varied than we imagine from a normal adult's point of view. One of the most common influences on a child's mind is the feeling of suppression brought about by a father's or mother's excessive punishment or abuse. This influence makes the child strive for release, and sometimes this is expressed in an attitude of psychological exclusion. Thus we find that some girls having high-tempered fathers have prototypes that exclude men because they are hightempered. Or boys suppressed by severe mothers may exclude women. This excluding attitude may of course be variously expressed: for instance, the child may become bashful, or on the other hand, he may become perverted sexually (which is simply another way of excluding women). Such perversions are not inherited, but arise from the environment surrounding the child in these years.

The early mistakes of the child are costly. And despite this fact the child receives little guidance. Parents do not know or will not confess to the child the results of their experiences, and the child must thus follow his own line.

Curiously enough we will find that no two children, even those born in the same family, grow up in the same situation. Even within

19

the same family the atmosphere that surrounds each individual child is quite particular. Thus the first child has notoriously a different set of circumstances from the other children. The first child is at first alone and is thus the center of attention. Once the second child is born, he finds himself dethroned and he does not like the change of situation. In fact it is quite a tragedy in his life that he has been in power and is so no longer. This sense of tragedy goes into the formation of his prototype and will crop out in his adult characteristics. As a matter of fact case histories show that such children always suffer downfall.

Another intra-family difference of environment is to be found in the different treatments accorded to boys and to girls. The usual case is for boys to be overvalued and the girls to be treated as if they could not accomplish anything. These girls will grow up always hesitating and in doubt. Throughout life they will hesitate too much, always remaining under the impression that only men are really able to accomplish anything.

The position of the second child is also characteristic and individual. He is in an entirely different position from that of the first child, inasmuch as for him there is always a pace-maker, moving along parallel with him. Usually the second child overcomes his pace-maker, and if we look for the cause we shall find simply that the older child was annoyed by having such a competitor and that the annoyance in the end affected his position in the family. The older child becomes frightened by the competition and does not do so well. He sinks more and more in the estimation of his parents, who begin to appreciate the second child. On the other hand the second child is always confronted by the pace-maker, and he is thus always in a race. All his characteristics will reflect this peculiar position in the family constellation. He shows rebellion and does not recognize power or authority.

History and legend recount numerous incidents of powerful youngest children. Joseph is a case in point: lie wanted to overcome all the others. The fact that a younger brother was born into the

20

family unknown to him years after he left home obyiously does not alter the situation. His position was that of the youngest. We find also the same description in all the fairy tales, in which the youngest child plays the leading role. We can see how these characteristics actually originate in early childhood and cannot be changed until the insight of the individual has increased. In order to readjust a child you must make him understand what happened in his first childhood. He must be made to understand that his prototype is erroneously influencing all the situations in his life.

A valuable tool for understanding the prototype and hence the nature of the individual is the study of old remembrances. All our knowledge and observation force us to the conclusion that our remembrances belong to the prototype. An illustration will make our point clear. Consider a child of the first type, one with imperfect organs with a weak stomach, let us say. If he remembers having seen something or heard something it will probably in some way concern eatables. Or take a child that is left-handed: his left-handedness will likewise affect his viewpoint. A person may tell you about his mother who pampered him, or about the birth of a younger child. He may tell you how he was beaten, if he had a high-tempered father, or how he was attacked if 'he was a hated child at school. All such indications are very valuable provided we learn the art of reading their significance.

The art of understanding old remembrances involves a very high power of sympathy, a power to identify oneself with the child in his childhood situation. It is only by such power of sympathy that we are able to understand the intimate significance in a child's life of the advent of a younger child in the family, or the impression made on a child's mind by the abuse of a hightempered father.

And while we are on the subject it cannot be overemphasized that nothing is gained by punishing, admonishing and preaching. Nothing is accomplished when neither the child nor the adult knows on which point the change has to be made. When the child does not understand, he becomes slyer and more cowardly. His prototype, however, cannot be changed by such punishment and preaching. It cannot be changed by mere experience of life, for the experience of life is already in accordance with the individual's personal scheme of apperception. It is only when we get at the basic personality that we accomplish any changes.

If we observe a family with badly developed children, we shall see that though they all seem to be intelligent (in the sense that if you ask a question they give the right answer), yet when we look for symptoms and expressions, they have a great feeling of inferiority. Intelligence of course is not necessarily common sense. The children have an entirely personal what we might term, a private mental attitude of the sort that one finds among neurotic persons. In a compulsion neurosis, for instance, the patient realizes the futility of always counting windows but cannot stop. One interested in useful things would never act this way. Private understanding and language are also characteristic of the insane. The insane never speak in the language of common sense, which represents the height of social interest.

If we contrast the judgment of common sense with private judgment, we shall find that the judgment of common sense is usually nearly right. By common sense we distinguish between good and bad, and while in a complicated situation we usually make mistakes, the mistakes tend to correct themselves through the very movement of common sense. But those who are always looking out for their own private interests cannot distinguish between right and wrong as readily as others. In fact they rather betray their inability, inasmuch as all their movements are transparent to the observer.

Consider for instance the commission of crimes. If we inquire about the intelligence, the understanding and the motive of a criminal, we shall find that the criminal always looks upon his crimes as both clever and heroic. He believes that he has achieved a goal of superiority namely, that he has become more clever than the police and is able to overcome others. He is thus a hero in his own mind, and does not see that his actions indicate something quite different, something very far from heroic. His lack of social interest, which

22

puts his activity on the useless side of life, is connected with a lack of courage, with cowardice, but he does not know this. Those who turn to the useless side of things are often afraid of darkness and isolation; they wish to be with others. This is cowardice and should be labeled as such. Indeed the best way to stop crime would be to convince everybody that crime is nothing but an expression of cowardice.

It is well known that some criminals when they approach the age of thirty will take a job, marry and become good citizens in later life. What happens? Consider a burglar. How can a thirty-year old burglar compete with a twenty-year old burglar? The latter is cleverer and more powerful. Moreover, at the age of thirty the criminal is forced to live differently from the way he lived before. As a result the profession of crime no longer pays the criminal and he finds it convenient to retire.

Another fact to be borne in mind in connection with criminals is that if we increase the punishments, so far from frightening the individual criminal, we merely help to increase his belief that he is a hero. We must not forget that the criminal lives in a self-centered world, a world in which one will never find true courage, self-confidence, communal sense, or understanding of common values. It is not possible for such persons to join a society. Neurotics seldom start a club, and it is an impossible feat for persons suffering from agoraphobia or for insane persons. Problem children or persons who commit suicide never make friends a fact for which the reason is never given. There is a reason, however: they never make friends because their early life took a self-centered direction. Their prototypes were oriented towards false goals and followed lines of direction on the useless side of life.

Let us now consider the program which Individual Psychology offers for the education and training of neurotic persons neurotic children, criminals, and persons who are drunkards and wish to escape by such means from the useful side of life.

In order to understand easily and quickly what is wrong, we begin by asking at what time the trouble originated. Usually the blame is laid on some new situation. But this is a mistake, for before this actual occurrence, our patient so we shall find upon investigation had not been well prepared for the situation. So long as he was in a favorable situation the mistakes of his prototype were not apparent, for each new situation is in the nature of an experiment to which he reacts according to the scheme of apperception created by his prototype. His responses are not mere reactions, they are creative and consistent with his goal, which is dominant throughout his life. Experience taught us early in our studies of Individual Psychology that we might exclude the importance of inheritance, as well as the importance of an isolated part. We see that the prototype answers experiences in accordance with its own scheme of apperception. And it is this scheme of apperception that we must work upon in order to produce any results.

This sums up the approach of Individual Psychology which has been developed in the last twenty-five years. As one may see, Individual Psychology has traveled a long way in a new direction. There are many psychologies and psychiatries in existence. One psychologist takes one direction, another another direction, and no one believes that the others are right. Perhaps the reader, too, should not rely on belief and faith. Let him compare. He will see that we cannot agree with what is called "drive" psychology (McDougall represents this tendency best in America), because in their "drives" too big a place is set aside for inherited tendencies. Similarly we cannot agree with the "conditioning" and "reactions" of Behaviorism. It is useless to construct the fate and character of an individual out of "drives" and "reactions" unless we understand the goal to which such movements are directed. Neither of these psychologies thinks in terms of individual goals.

It is true that when the word "goal" is mentioned, the reader is likely to have a hazy impression. The idea needs to be concretized. Now in the last analysis to have a goal is to aspire to be like God, But to be like God is of course the ultimate goal the goal of goals, if we may use the term. Educators should be cautious in attempting to educate themselves and their children to be like God. As a matter of fact we find that the child in his development substitutes a more concrete and immediate goal. Children look for the strongest person in their environment and make him their model or their goal. It may be the father, or perhaps the mother, for we find that even a boy may be influenced to imitate his mother if she seems the strongest person. Later on they want to be coachmen because they believe the coachman is the strongest person.

When children first conceive such a goal they behave, feel and dress like the coachman and take on all the characteristics consistent with the goal. But let the policeman lift a finger, and the coachman becomes nothing... Later on the ideal may become the doctor or the teacher. For the teacher can punish the child and thus he arouses his respect as a strong person.

The child has a choice of concrete symbols in selecting his goal, and we find that the goal he chooses is really an index of his social interests. A boy, asked what he wanted to be in later life, said, "I want to be a hangman." This displays a lack of social interest. The boy wished to be the master of life and death a role which belongs to God. He wished to be more powerful than society, and he was thus headed for the useless life. The goal of being a doctor is also fashioned around the God-like desire of being master of life and death, but here the goal is realized through social service.

CHAPTER TWO

THE INFERIORITY COMPLEX

THE use of the terms "consciousness" and "unconsciousness" to designate distinctive factors is incorrect in the practice of Individual Psychology. Consciousness and unconsciousness move together in the same direction and are not contradictions, as is so often believed. What is more, there is no definite line of demarcation between them. It is merely a question of discovering the purpose of their joint movement. It is impossible to decide on what is conscious and what is not until the whole connection has been obtained. This connection is revealed in the prototype, that pattern of life which we analyzed in the last chapter.

A case history will serve to illustrate the intimate connection between conscious and unconscious life. A married man, forty years old, suffered from one anxiety a desire to jump out of the window. He was always struggling against this desire, but aside from this he was quite well. He had friends, a good position, and lived with his wife happily. His case is inexplicable except in terms of the collaboration of consciousness and unconsciousness. Consciously he had the feeling that he must jump out of a window. Nonetheless he lived on, and in fact he never even attempted to jump out of a window. The reason for this is that there was another side to his life, a side in which a struggle against his desire to commit suicide played an important part. As a result of the collaboration of this unconscious side of his being with his consciousness, he came out victorious. In fact in his "style of life" to use a term about which we shall have more to say in a later chapter he was a conqueror who had attained the goal of superiority. The reader might ask how could this man feel superior when he had this conscious tendency to commit suicide? The answer is that there was something in his being that was fighting his battle against his suicidal tendency. It is his success in this battle that made him a conqueror and a superior being. Objectively his struggle for superiority was conditioned by his own weakness, as is very often the case with persons who in one way or another feel inferior. But the important thing is that in his own private battle his striving for superiority, his striving to live and to conquer, came out ahead of his sense of inferiority and desire to die and this despite the fact that the latter was expressed in his conscious life and the former in his unconscious life.

Let us see if the development of this man's prototype bears out our theory. Let us analyze his childhood remembrances. At an early age, we learn, he had trouble at school. He did not like other boys and wanted to run away from them. Nonetheless he collected all his powers to stay arid face them. In other words we can already perceive an effort on his part to overcome his weakness. He faced his problem and conquered.

If we analyze our patient's character, we shall see that his one aim in life was to overcome fear and anxiety. In this aim his conscious ideas cooperated with his unconscious ones and formed a unity. Now a person who does not see the human being as a unity might believe that this patient was not superior and was not successful. He might think him to be only an ambitious person, one who wanted to struggle and fight but who was at bottom a coward. Such a view would be erroneous, however, since it would not take into consideration all the facts in the case and interpret them with reference to the unity of a human life. Our whole psychology, our whole understanding or striving to understand individuals would be futile and useless if we could not be sure that the human being is a unity. If we presupposed two sides without relation to one another it would be impossible to see life as a complete entity.

In addition to regarding an individual's life as a unity, we must also take it together with its context of social relations. Thus children when first born are weak, and their weakness makes it necessary for other persons to care for them. Now the style or the pattern of a child's life cannot be understood without reference to the persons who look after him and who make up for his inferiority. The child has interlocking relations with the mother and family which could never be understood if we confined our analysis to the periphery of the child's physical being in space. The individuality of the child cuts across his physical individuality, it involves a whole context of social relations.

What applies to the child applies also, to a certain extent, to men as a whole. The weakness which is responsible for the child's living in a family group is paralleled by the weakness which drives men to live in society. All persons feel inadequate in certain situations. They feel overwhelmed by the difficulties of life and are incapable of meeting them single-handed. Hence one of the strongest tendencies in man has been to form groups in order that he may live as a member of a society and not as an isolated individual. This social life has without doubt been a great help to him in overcoming his feeling of inadequacy and inferiority. We know that this is the case with animals, where the weaker species always live in groups in order that their combined powers might help to meet their individual needs. Thus a herd of buffaloes can defend themselves against wolves. One buffalo alone would find this impossible, but in a group they stick their heads together and fight with their feet until they are saved. On the other hand, gorillas, lions and tigers can live isolated because nature has given them the means of self-protection. A human being has not their great strength, their claws, nor their teeth, and so cannot live apart. Thus we find that the beginning of social life lies in the weakness of the individual.

Because of this fact we cannot expect to find that the abilities and faculties of all human beings in society are equal. But a society that is rightly adjusted will not be behindhand in supporting the abilities of the individuals who compose it. This is an important point to grasp, since otherwise we would be led to suppose that individuals have to be judged entirely on their inherited abilities. As a matter of fact an individual who might be deficient in certain faculties if he lived in an isolated condition could well compensate for his lacks in a rightly organized society.

Let us suppose that our individual insufficiencies are inherited. It then becomes the aim of psychology to train people to live well with others, in order to help decrease the effect of their natural disabilities. The history of social progress tells the story of how men co-operated in order to overcome deficiencies and lacks. Everybody knows that language is a social invention, but few people realize that individual deficiency was the mother of that invention. This truth, however, is illustrated in the early behavior of children. When their desires are not being satisfied, they want to gain attention and they try to do so by some sort of language. But if a child should not need to gain attention, he would not try to speak at all. This is the case in the first few months, when the child's mother supplies everything that the child wishes before it speaks. There are cases on record of children who did not speak until six years of age because it was never necessary for them to do so. The same truth is illustrated in the case of a particular child of deaf and dumb parents. When he fell and hurt himself he cried, but he cried without noise. He knew that noise would be useless as his parents could not hear him. Therefore he made the appearance of crying in order to gain the attention of his parents, but it was noiseless.

We see therefore that we must always look at the whole social context of the facts we study. We must look at the social environment in order to understand the particular "goal of superiority" an individual chooses. We must look at the social situation, too, in order to understand a particular maladjustment. Thus many persons are mal-adjusted because they find it impossible to make the normal contact with others by means of language. The stammerer is a case in point. If we examine the stammerer we shall see that since the beginning of his life he was never socially well adjusted. He did not want to join in activities, and he did not want friends or comrades. His language development needed association with others, but he did not want to associate. Therefore his stammering continued. There are really two tendencies in stammerers one to associate with others, and another that makes them seek isolation for themselves.

29

Later in life, among adult persons not living a social life, we find that they cannot speak in public and have a tendency to stage fright. This is because they regard their audiences as enemies. They have a feeling of inferiority when confronted by a seemingly hostile and dominating audience. The fact is that only when a person trusts himself and his audience can he speak well, and only then will he not have stage fright.

The feeling of inferiority and the problem of social training are thus intimately connected. Just as the feeling of inferiority arises from a social maladjustment, so social training is the basic method by which we can all overcome our feelings of inferiority.

There is a direct connection between social training and common sense. When we say that people solve their difficulties by common sense, we have in mind the pooled intelligence of the social group. On the other hand, as we indicated in the last chapter, persons who act with a private language and a private understanding manifest an abnormality. The insane, the neurotics and the criminals are of this type. We find that certain things are not interesting to them people, institutions, the social norms make no appeal to them. And yet it is through these things that the road to their salvation lies.

In working with such persons our task is to make social facts appeal to them. Nervous persons always feel justified if they show good will. But more than good will is needed. We must teach them that it is what they actually accomplish, what they actually give, that matters in society.

While the feeling of inferiority and the striving for superiority are universal, it would be a mistake to regard this fact as indicating that all men are equal. Inferiority and superiority are the general conditions which govern the behavior of men, but besides these conditions there are differences in bodily strength, in health, and in environment. For that reason different mistakes are made by individuals in the same given conditions. If we examine children we shall see that there is no one absolutely fixed and right manner for them to respond. They respond in their own individual ways.

30

They strive towards a better style of life, but they all strive in their own way, making their own mistakes and their own type of approximations to success.

Let us analyze some of the variations and peculiarities of individuals. Let us take, for example, left-handed children. There are children who may never know that they are left-handed because they have been so carefully trained in the use of the right hand. At first they are clumsy and imperfect with the right hand, and they are scolded, criticised and derided. It is an error to deride, but both hands should be trained. A left-handed child can be recognized in the cradle because his left hand moves more than his right. In later life he may feel that he is burdened because of the imperfection of his right hand. On the other hand, he often develops a greater interest in his right hand and arm, which interest is manifested, for example, in drawing, writing, etc. In fact it is not surprising to find that later in life such a child is better trained than a normal child. Because he has had to get interested, he has gotten up earlier, so to speak, and thus his imperfection has led him to more careful training. This is often a great advantage in developing artistic talent and ability. A child in such a position is usually ambitious and fights to overcome his limitations. Sometimes, however, if the struggle is a serious one, he may become envious or jealous of others and thus develop a greater feeling of inferiority which is more difficult to overcome than in normal cases. Through constant struggling a child may become a fighting child or a fighting adult, always striving with the fixed idea in mind that he ought not to be clumsy and deficient. Such an individual is more burdened than others.

Children strive, make mistakes, and develop in various ways according to the prototypes they formed in the first; four or five years of life. The goal of each is different. One child may want to be a painter, while another may wish himself out of this world where he is a misfit. We may know how he can overcome his imperfection, but he does not know it, and all too often the facts are not explained to him in the right way.

31

Many children have imperfect eyes, ears, lungs or stomachs, and we find their interest stimulated in the direction of the imperfection. A curious instance of this is revealed in the case of a man who suffered from attacks of asthma only when he came home at night from the office. He was a man of forty-five, married, and with a good position. He was asked why the attacks always occurred after he came home from the office. He explained, "You see, my wife is very materialistic and I am idealistic, hence we do not agree. When I come home I would like to be quiet, to enjoy myself at home, but my wife wants to go into society and so she complains about remaining at home. Whereupon I get into a bad temper and start to suffocate."

Why did this man suffocate: why did he not vomit? The fact is he was only being true to his prototype. It seems that as a child he had to be bandaged for some weakness and this tight binding affected his breathing and made him very uncomfortable. He had a maid servant, however, who liked him and would sit beside him and console him. All her interest was in him and not in herself. She thus gave him the impression that he would always be amused and consoled. When he was four years old the nurse went away to a wedding and he accompanied her to the station crying very bitterly. After the nurse had left he said to his mother, "The world has no more interest for me now that my nurse has gone away."

Hence we see him in manhood as in the years of his prototype, looking for an ideal person who would always amuse him and console him and be interested in him alone. The trouble was not too little air but the fact that he was not being amused and consoled at all times. Naturally, to find a person who will always amuse you is not easy. He always wanted to rule the whole situation and to a certain degree it helped him when he succeeded. Thus when he took to suffocating, his wife stopped wanting to go to the theatre or into society. He had then obtained his "goal of superiority."

Consciously this man was always right and proper, but in his mind he had the desire to be the conqueror. He wanted to make his wife

32

what he called idealistic instead of materialistic. We should suspect such a man of motives different from those on the surface....

We often see children with imperfect eyes take more of an interest in visual things. They develop a keen faculty in this way. We see Gustav Freitag, a great poet who had poor, astigmatic eyes, accomplishing much. Poets and painters often have trouble with their eyes. But this in itself often creates greater interest. Freitag said about himself: "Because my eyes were different from those of other people, it seems that I was compelled to use and train my fantasy. I do not know that this has helped me to be a great writer, but in any case as a result of my eyesight it has come about that I can see better in fantasy than others in reality."

If we examine the personalities of geniuses we shall often find poor eyes or some other deficiency. In the history of all ages even the gods have had some deficiency such as blindness in one or both eyes. The fact that there are geniuses who though nearly blind are yet able to understand better than others the differences in lines, shadows and colors shows what can be done with afflicted children if their problems are properly understood.

Some people are more interested in eatables than others. Because of this they are always discussing what they can and what they cannot cat. Usually such persons have had a hard time at the beginning of life in the matter of eating and so have developed more interest in it than others. They had probably been told constantly by a watchful mother what they could and could not eat. Such persons have to train to overcome the imperfections of their stomachs, and they become vitally interested in what they will have for lunch, dinner or breakfast. As a result of their constant thought about eating they sometimes develop the art of cookery or become experts on questions of diet.

At times, however, a weakness of the stomach or the intestines causes people to look for a substitute for eating. Sometimes this substitute is money, and such persons become miserly or great money-making bankers. They often strive extremely hard to collect

33

money, training themselves for this purpose day and night. They never stop thinking of their business, a fact which may sometimes give them a great advantage over others in similar walks of life. And it is interesting to note that we often hear of rich men suffering from stomach trouble.

Let us remind ourselves at this point of the connection frequently made between body and mind. A given defect does not always lead to the same result. There is no necessary cause and effect relation between a physical imperfection and a bad style of life. For the physical imperfection we can often give good treatment in the form of right nutrition and thereby partly obviate the physical situation. But it is not the physical defect which causes the bad results: it is the patient's attitude which is responsible. That is why for the individual psychologist mere physical defects or exclusive physical causality does not exist, but only mistaken attitudes towards physical situations. Also that is why the individual psychologist seeks to foster a striving against the feeling of inferiority during the development of the prototype.

Sometimes we see a person impatient because he cannot wait to overcome difficulties. Whenever we see persons constantly in motion, with strong tempers and passions, we can always conclude that they are persons with a great feeling of inferiority. A person who knows he can overcome his difficulties will not be impatient. On the other hand he may not always accomplish what is necessary. Arrogant, impertinent, fighting children also indicate a great feeling of inferiority. It is our task in their case to look for the reasons for the difficulties they have in order to prescribe the treatment. We should never criticise or punish mistakes in the style of life of the prototype.

We can recognize these prototype traits among children in very peculiar ways in their unusual interests, in their scheming and striving to surpass others, and in building toward the goal of superiority. There is a type that does not trust himself in movement and expression. He prefers to exclude others as far as possible. He prefers not to go where he is confronted with new situations but to

34

stay in the little circle in which he feels sure. In school, in life, in society, in marriage he does the same. He is always hoping to accomplish much in his little place in order to arrive at a goal of superiority. We find this trait among many human beings. They all forget that to accomplish results, one must be prepared to meet all situations. Everything must be faced. If one eliminates certain situations and certain persons, one has only private intelligence to justify oneself, and this is not enough. One needs all the renovating winds of social contact and common sense.

If a philosopher wants to accomplish his work, he cannot always go to lunch or dinner with others, for he needs to be alone for long periods of time in order to collect his ideas and use the right method. But later on he must grow through contact with society. This contact is an important part of his development. And so when we meet with such a person we must remember his two requirements. We must remember, too, that he can be useful or useless and should therefore look carefully for the difference between useful and useless behavior.

The key to the entire social process is to be found in the fact that persons are always striving to find a situation in which they excel. Thus children who have a great feeling of inferiority want to exclude stronger children and play with weaker children whom they can rule and domineer. This is an abnormal and pathological expression of the feeling of inferiority, for it is important to realize that it is not the sense of inferiority which matters but the degree and character of it.

The abnormal feeling of inferiority has acquired the name of "inferiority complex." But complex is not the correct word for this feeling of inferiority that permeates the whole personality. It is more than a complex, it is almost a disease whose ravages vary under different circumstances. Thus we sometimes do not notice the feeling of inferiority when a person is on his job because he feels sure of his work. On the other hand he may not be sure of himself in society or in his relations with the opposite sex, and in this way we are able to discover his true psychological situation.

35

We notice mistakes in a greater degree in a tense or difficult situation. It is in the difficult or new situation that the prototype appears rightly, and in fact the difficult situation is nearly always the new one. That is why, as we said in the first chapter, the expression of the degree of social interest appears in a new social situation.

If we put a child to school we may observe his social interest there just as in general social life. We can see whether he mixes with his fellows or avoids them. If we see hyperactive, sly, clever children, we must look into their minds to find the reasons. And if we see some go forward only conditionally or hesitatingly, we must be on the lookout for the same characteristics to be revealed later on in society, life and marriage.

We always meet persons who say, "I would do this in this way," "I would take that job," "I would fight that man, ...but.. , !" All such statements are a sign of a great feeling of inferiority, and in fact if we read them this way we get a new light on certain emotions, such as doubt. We recognize that a person in doubt usually remains in doubt and accomplishes nothing. However, when a person says "I won't" he will probably act accordingly.

The psychologist, if he looks closely can often see contradictions in men. Such contradictions may be considered as a sign of a feeling of inferiority. But we must also observe the movements of a person who constitutes our problem on hand. Thus, his approach, his way of meeting people, may be poor, and we must observe if he comes towards persons with a hesitating step and bodily attitude. This hesitation will often be expressed in other situations of life. There are many persons who take one step forward and one backward a sign of a great feeling of inferiority.

Our whole task is to train such persons away from their hesitating attitude. The proper treatment for such persons is to encourage them never to discourage them. We must make them understand that they are capable of facing difficulties and solving the problems of life. This is the only way to build self-confidence, and this is the only way the feeling of inferiority should be treated.

CHAPTER THREE

THE SUPERIORITY COMPLEX

IN the last chapter we discussed the inferiority complex and its relation to the general feeling of inferiority which all of us share and struggle against. Now we have to turn to the inverse topic, the superiority complex.

We have seen how every symptom of an individual's life is expressed in a movement in a progress. Thus the symptom may be said to have a past and a future. Now the future is tied up with our striving and with our goal, while the past represents the state of inferiority or inadequacy which we are trying to overcome. That is why in an inferiority complex we are interested in the beginning, while in a superiority complex we are more interested in the continuity, in the progression of the movement itself. Moreover, the two complexes are naturally related. We should not be astonished if in the cases where we see an inferiority complex we find a superiority complex more or less hidden. On the other hand, if we inquire into a superiority complex and study its continuity, we can always find a more or less hidden inferiority complex.

We must bear in mind of course that the word complex as attached to inferiority and superiority merely represents an exaggerated condition of the sense of inferiority and the striving for superiority. If we look at things this way it takes away the apparent paradox of two contradictory tendencies, the inferiority complex and the superiority complex, existing in the same individual. For it is obvious that as normal sentiments the striving for superiority and the feeling of inferiority are naturally complementary. We should not strive to be superior and to succeed if we did not feel a certain lack in our present condition. Now inasmuch as the so-called complexes develop out of the natural sentiments, there is no more contradiction in them than in the sentiments.

37

The striving for superiority never ceases. It constitutes in fact the mind, the psyche of the individual. As we have said, life is the attainment of a goal or form, and it is the striving for superiority which sets the attainment of form into motion. It is like a stream which drags along all the material it can find. If we look at lazy children and see their lack of activity, their lack of interest in anything, we should say that they do not seem to be moving. But nonetheless we find in them a desire to be superior, a desire which makes them say, "If I were not so lazy, I could be president." They are moving and striving conditionally, so to speak. They hold a high opinion of themselves and take the view that they could accomplish much on the useful side of life, if...! This is lying, of course it's fiction, but as we all know, mankind is very often satisfied with fiction. And this is especially true of persons who lack courage. They content themselves quite well with fiction. They do not feel very strong and so they always make detours they always want to escape difficulties. Through this escape, through this avoiding of battle they get a feeling of being much stronger and cleverer than they really are.

We see children who start stealing suffering from the feeling of superiority. They believe they are deceiving others; that others do not know they are stealing. Thus they are richer with little effort. This same feeling is very pronounced among criminals who have the idea that they are superior heroes.

We have already spoken of this trait from another aspect as a manifestation of private intelligence. It is not common or social sense. If a murderer thinks himself a hero, it is a private idea. He is lacking in courage since he wants to arrange matters so that he escapes the solution of the problems of life. Criminality is thus the result of a superiority complex and not the expression of fundamental and original viciousness.

We see similar symptoms appearing among neurotic persons. For example they suffer from sleeplessness and so are not strong enough next day to comply with the demands of their occupations. Because of sleeplessness they feel that they cannot be required to

38

work because they are not equal to doing what they could accomplish. They lament, "What could I not do if I could only get my sleep I"

We see this also among depressed persons suffering from anxiety. Their anxiety makes them tyrants over others. In fact they use their anxiety to rule others, for they must always have people with them, they must be accompanied wherever they go, etc. The companions are made to live their lives in accordance with the demands of the depressed person.

Melancholy and insane persons are always the center of attention in the family. In them we see the power wielded by the inferiority complex. They complain that they feel weak and are losing weight, etc., but nonetheless they are the strongest of all. They dominate healthy persons. This fact should not surprise us, for in our culture weakness can be quite strong and powerful. (In fact if we were to ask ourselves who is the strongest person in our culture, the logical answer would be, the baby. The baby rules and cannot be dominated.)

Let us study the connection between the superiority complex and inferiority. Let us take for example a problem child with a superiority complex a child that is impertinent, arrogant and pugnacious. We shall find that he always wants to appear greater than he really is. We all know how children with temper tantrums want to control others by getting a sudden attack. Why are they so impatient? Because they are not sure they are strong enough to attain their goal. They feel inferior. We will always discover in fighting, aggressive children an inferiority complex and a desire to overcome it. It is as if they were trying to lift themselves on their toes in order to appear greater and to gain by this easy method success, pride and superiority,

We have to find methods of treatment for such children. They act that way because they do not see the coherence of life. They do not see the natural order of things. We should not censure them because they do not want to see it, for if we confront them with the

39

question, they will always insist that they do not feel inferior but superior. We must therefore in a friendly manner explain to them our point of view and get them gradually to understand.

If a person is a show-off it is only because he feels inferior, because he does not feel strong enough to compete with others on the useful side of life. That is why he stays on the useless side. He is not in harmony with society. He is not socially adjusted, and he does not know how to solve the social problems of life. And so we always find a struggle between him and his parents and teachers during his childhood. In such cases the situation must be understood and also made understandable to the children.

We see the same combination of inferiority and superiority complexes in neurotic illnesses. The neurotic frequently expresses his superiority complex but does not see his inferiority complex. The case history of a compulsion neurotic is very illuminating in this regard. There was a young girl in close association with an elder sister who was very charming and much esteemed. This fact is significant at the outset, for if one person out of a family is more outstanding than the others, the latter will suffer. This is always so, whether the favored individual be the father, one of the children, or the mother. A very difficult situation is created for the other members of the family, and sometimes they feel they cannot bear it.

Now we will find among these other children that they all have an inferiority complex and are striving toward a superiority complex. So long as they are interested not only in themselves but in others, they will solve their problems of life satisfactorily. But if their inferiority complex is clearly marked, they find themselves living, as it were, in an enemy country always looking out for their own interests rather than for those of others, and thus not having the right amount of communal sense. They approach the social questions of life with a feeling that is not conducive to their solution. And so, seeking relief, they go over to the useless side of life. We know that this is not really relief, but it seems like relief not to solve questions but to be supported by others. They are like beggars, who are being supported by others and who feel

40

comfortable neurotically exploiting their weakness. It seems to be a trait of human nature that when individuals both children and adults feel weak, they cease to be interested socially but strive for superiority. They want to solve the problems of life in such a way as to obtain personal superiority without any admixture of social interest. As long as a person strives for superiority and tempers it with social interest, he is on the useful side of life and can accomplish good. But if he lacks social interest, he is not really prepared for the solution of the problems of life. In this category should be put, as we have already said, the problem children, the insane, the criminals, those who commit suicide, etc.

Now this girl of whom we started to speak grew up outside of a favorable circle and felt herself restricted. If she had been socially interested, and had understood what we understand, she could have developed along another line. She began to study to be a musician, but she was always at such tension, due to the inferiority complex caused by always thinking of her preferred sister, that she was blocked here too. When she was twenty her sister married and so she began to look for marriage in order to compete with her sister. In this way she was getting in deeper, and drifting more and more from the healthy, useful side of life. She developed the idea that she was a bad, bad girl, and possessed magic power which could send a person to hell.

We see this magic power as a superiority complex, but she on the other hand complained, just as we sometimes hear rich men complain of how bad their fate is to be rich men. Not only did she feel that she had the god-like power of sending people to hell, but at times she got the impression that she could and ought to save these people. Of course both of these claims were ridiculous, but by means of this system of fiction she assured herself of possessing a power that was higher than her preferred sister's. She could overcome her sister only by this game. And so she complained that she had this power, for the more she complained about it the more plausible it was that she actually possessed it. If she had laughed about it, the claim of power would have been questionable. Only by

41

complaining could she feel happy with her lot. We see here how a superiority complex may sometimes be hidden, not recognized as present, yet existing in fact as a compensation for the inferiority complex.

The older sister of whom we shall now speak was very much favored, for at one time she was the only child, much pampered, and the center of attention in the family. Three years later there arrived a younger sister, which fact changed the whole situation for the older girl. Formerly she had always been alone, the center of attention. Now she was suddenly thrown out of this position. As a result she became a fighting child. But there can be fighting only where there are weaker companions. A fighting child is not really courageous he fights only against weaker persons. If the environment is strong, then instead of becoming pugnacious, a child becomes peevish, or depressed, and is likely to be less appreciated in the home circle for this reason.

In such cases the older child feels she is not as dearly loved as before, and she sees the manifestations of the changed attitude as a confirmation of her view. She considers her mother the most guilty inasmuch as it is she who has brought this other girl into the home. Thus we can understand her directing attacks against her mother.

The baby, on the other hand, has to be watched, observed, pampered as all babies are, and is thus in a favorable position. Therefore she does not need to exert herself, does not need to fight. She develops as a very sweet, very soft and very much beloved creature the center of the family. Sometimes virtue in the form of obedience may conquer!

Now let us examine and see if this sweetness, softness and kindness was on the useful side of life or not. We may presuppose that she was so amenable and tractable only because she was so pampered. But our civilization does not regard pampered children with favor. Sometimes the father realizes this and wants to end this state of affairs. Sometimes the school comes into the situation. The position of such a child is always in danger and for this reason the pampered child feels inferior. We do not notice this feeling of inferiority among pampered children so long as they are in a favorable situation, but the moment an unfavorable situation arises we see these children either breaking down and becoming depressed or developing a superiority complex.

The superiority complex and inferiority complex agree on one point, namely, that they are always on the useless side. We can never find an arrogant, impertinent child, one with a superiority complex, on the useful side of life.

When these pampered children go to school, they are no longer in a favorable situation. From that moment on we see them adopting a hesitating attitude in life and never finishing anything. So it was with the younger sister of whom we first spoke. She began to learn to sew, to play the piano, etc., but after a short time she stopped. At the same time she lost interest in society, did not like to go out any more and felt depressed. She felt herself overshadowed by her sister with her more agreeable characteristics. Pier hesitating attitude made her weaker and caused a deterioration of her character.

Later in life she hesitated in the matter of occupations and never finished anything. She also hesitated in love and marriage, despite her desire to compete with her sister. When she reached thirty she looked around and found a man who was suffering from tuberculosis. Of course we can readily see that this selection would be opposed by her parents. In this case it was not necessary for her to stop action, for her parents stopped the action, and the marriage did not take place. A year later she married a man thirty-five years her senior. Now as such a man is not thought to be a man any more, this marriage which was not a marriage seemed useless. We often find an expression of an inferiority complex in the selection of a much older person for marriage or in the selection of a person who cannot be married; for example, a married man 01 woman. There is always a suspicion of cowardice when there are hindrances. Because this girl did not justify her feeling of superiority in

43

marriage, she found another way of acquiring a superiority complex.

She insisted that the most important thing in this world is duty. She had to wash herself all the time. If anybody or anything touched her, she had to wash again. In this way she became wholly isolated. As a matter of fact her hands were as dirty as they could be. The reason was obvious: because of her continual washing she acquired a very rough skin that collected dirt in great quantities.

Now all this looks like an inferiority complex, but she felt herself to be the only pure person in the world and was continually criticising and accusing others because they did not have her washing mania. So she played her role as in a pantomime. She had always wanted to be superior and now in a fictitious way she was. She was the purest person in the world. So we see that her inferiority complex had become a superiority complex, very distinctly expressed.

We see the same phenomenon in megalomaniacs who believe themselves to be Jesus Christ or an emperor. Such a person is on the useless side of life and plays his role almost as if it were true. He is isolated in life, and we shall find, if we go back to his past, that he felt inferior and that, in a worthless way, he developed a superiority complex.

There is the case of a boy of fifteen who entered an asylum for the insane because of his hallucinations. At that time, which was before the war, he fancied that the emperor of Austria was dead. This was not true, but he claimed that the emperor had appeared to him in a dream demanding that he lead the Austrian army against the enemy. And he a little undersized boy! He would not be convinced when he was shown the newspapers, which reported that the emperor was stopping at his castle or that he had been out driving in his car. He insisted that the emperor was dead and had appeared to him in a dream.

At that time Individual Psychology was trying to find out the importance of positions in sleep in indicating a person's feeling of

44

superiority or inferiority. One can see that such information might prove useful. Some persons lie in bed in a curved line like a hedgehog, covering their heads with the covers. This expresses an inferiority complex. Can we believe such a person to be courageous? Or if we see a person stretched out straight, can we believe him weak or bent in life? Both in a literal and metaphorical way he will appear great, as he does in sleep. It has been observed that persons who sleep on their stomachs are stubborn and pugnacious.

This boy was examined in an attempt to find correlations between his waking behavior and his positions in sleep. It was found that he slept with arms crossed on his breast, like Napoleon. As we all know the pictures show Napoleon with his arms in such a position. Next day the boy was asked, "Do you know somebody of whom this position reminds you?" He answered, "Yes, my teacher." The discovery was a little disturbing until it was suggested that the teacher might be like Napoleon. This proved to be the case. Moreover, the boy had loved this teacher and wanted to be a teacher like him. But for lack of funds with which to assure him an education, his family had to put him to work in a restaurant where the patrons had all derided him because he was undersized. He could not bear this and wanted to escape from this feeling of humiliation. But he escaped to the useless side of life.

We are able to understand what happened in the case of this boy. In the beginning he had an inferiority complex because he was undersized and hence derided by the guests in the restaurant. But he was constantly striving for superiority. He wanted to be a teacher. But because he was blocked in attaining this occupation, he found another goal of superiority by making a detour to the useless side of life. He became superior in sleep and dreams.

Thus we see that the goal of superiority may be on the useless or useful side of life. If a person is benevolent, for instance, it may mean either of two things it may mean that he is socially adjusted and wants to help, or else it may mean simply that he wants to boast. The psychologist meets with many whose main goal is to boast. There is the case of a boy who was not very accomplished in school; in fact he was so bad that he became a truant and stole things, but he was always boastful. He did these things because of his inferiority complex. He wanted to accomplish results in some line be it only the line of cheap vanity. Thus he stole money and presented prostitutes with flowers and other gifts. One day he drove a car far away to a little town and there he demanded a carriage and six horses. He rode all through the town in state until he was arrested. In all his behavior his great striving was to appear greater than others and greater than he really was.

A similar tendency may be remarked in the behavior of criminals the tendency to claim easy success, which we have already discussed in another connection. The New York newspapers some time ago reported how a burglar broke into the home of some schoolteachers and had a discussion with them. The burglar told the women they did not know how much trouble there was in ordinary honest occupations. It was much easier to be a burglar than to work. This man had escaped to the useless side of life. But by taking this road he had developed a certain superiority complex. He felt stronger than the women, particularly since he was armed and they were not. But did he realize that he was a coward? We know he is because we see him as a person who had escaped his inferiority complex by going over to the useless side of life. He thought himself a hero, however, and not a coward.

Some types turn to suicide and desire in this way to throw off the whole world with its difficulties. They seem not to care for life and so feel superior, although they are really cowards. We see that a superiority complex is a second phase. It is a compensation for the inferiority complex, we must always try to find the organic connection the connection which may seem to be a contradiction but which is quite in the course of human nature, as we have already shown. Once this connection is found we are in a position to treat both the inferiority and superiority complexes.

We should not conclude the general subject of inferiority and superiority complexes without saying a few words as to the relation

46

of these complexes to normal persons. Everyone, as we have said, has a feeling of inferiority. But the feeling of inferiority is not a disease, it is rather a stimulant to healthy normal striving and development. It becomes a pathological condition only when the sense of inadequacy overwhelms the individual, and so far from stimulating him to useful activity, makes him depressed and incapable of development. Now the superiority complex is one of the ways which a person with an inferiority complex may use as a method of escape from his difficulties. He assumes that he is superior when he is not, and this false success compensates him for the state of inferiority which he cannot bear. The normal person does not have a superiority complex, he does not even have a sense of superiority. He has the striving to be superior in the sense that we all have ambition to be successful, but so long as this striving is expressed in work it does not lead to false valuations, which is at the root of mental disease.

CHAPTER FOUR

THE STYLE OF LIFE

IF we look at a pine tree growing in the valley we will notice that it grows differently from one on top of a mountain. It is the same kind of a tree, a pine, but there are two distinct styles of life. Its style on top of the mountain is different from its style when growing in the valley. The style of life of a tree is the individuality of a tree expressing itself and moulding itself in an environment. We recognize a style when we see it against a background of an environment different from what we expect, for then we realize that every tree has a life pattern and is not merely a mechanical reaction to the environment.

It is much the same way with human beings. We see the style of life under certain conditions of environment and it is our task to analyze its exact relation to the existing circumstances, inasmuch as mind changes with alteration of the environment. As long as a person is in a favorable situation we cannot see his style of life clearly. In new situations, however, where he is confronted with difficulties, the style of life appears clearly and distinctly. A trained psychologist could perhaps understand a style of life of a human being even in a favorable situation, but it becomes apparent to everybody when the human subject is put into unfavorable or difficult situations.

Now life, being something more than a game, does not lack difficulties. There are always situations in which human beings find themselves confronted with difficulties. It is while the subject is confronted with these difficulties that we must study him and find out his different movements and characteristic distinguishing marks. As we have previously said, the style of life is a unity because it has grown out of the difficulties of early life and out of the striving for a goal.

But we are interested not so much in the past as in the future. And in order to understand a person's future we must understand his style of life. Even if we understand instincts, stimuli, drive, etc., we cannot predict what must happen. Some psychologists indeed try to reach conclusions by noting certain instincts, impressions or traumas, but on closer examination it will be found that all these elements presuppose a consistent style of life. Thus whatever stimulates, stimulates only to save and fix a style of life.

How does the notion of the style of life tie up with what we have discussed in previous chapters? We have seen how human beings with weak organs, because they face difficulties and feel insecure, suffer from a feeling or complex of inferiority. But as human beings cannot endure this for long, the inferiority feeling stimulates them, as we have seen, to movement and action. This results in a person having a goal. Now Individual Psychology has long called the consistent movement toward this goal a plan of life. But because this name has sometimes led to mistakes among students, it is now called a style of life.

Because an individual has a style of life, it is possible to predict his future sometimes just on the basis of talking to him and having him answer questions. It is like looking at the fifth act of a drama, where all the mysteries are solved. We can make predictions in this way because we know the phases, the difficulties and the questions of life. Thus from experience and knowledge of a few facts we can tell what will happen to children who always separate themselves from others, who are looking for support, who are pampered and who hesitate in approaching situations. What happens in the case of a person whose goal it is to be supported by others? Hesitating, he stops or escapes the solution of the questions of life. We know how he can hesitate, stop, or escape, because we have seen the same thing happen a thousand times. We know that he does not want to proceed alone but wants to be pampered. He wants to stay far away from the great problems of life, and he occupies himself with useless things rather than struggle with the useful ones. He lacks social interests, and as a result he may develop into a problem child, a neurotic, a criminal or a suicide that final escape. All these things are now better understood than formerly.

We realize, for instance, that in looking for the style of a life of a human being we may use the normal style of life as a basis for measurement.

We use the socially adjusted human being as a stand, and we can measure the variations from the normal.

At this point perhaps it would be helpful to show how we determine the normal style of life and how on the basis of it we understand mistakes and peculiarities. But before we discuss this we ought to mention that we do not count types in such studies. We do not consider human beings types because every human being has an individual style of life. Just as one cannot find two leaves of a tree absolutely identical, so one cannot find two human beings absolutely alike. Nature is so rich and the possibilities of stimuli, instincts and mistakes are so numerous, that it is not possible for two persons to be exactly identical. If we speak of types, therefore, it is only as an intellectual device to make more understandable the similarities of individuals. We can judge better if we postulate an intellectual classification like a type and study its special peculiarities. However, in doing so we do not commit ourselves to using the same classification at all times; we use the classification which is most useful for bringing out a particular similarity. People who take types and classifications seriously, once they put a person in a pigeonhole, do not see how he can be put into any other classifications

An illustration will make our point clear. For instance when we speak of a type of individual not socially adjusted, we refer to one who leads a barren life without any social interests. This is one way of classifying individuals, and perhaps it is the most important way. But consider the individual, whose interest, however limited, is centered on visual things. Such a person differs entirely from one whose interests are largely concentrated on things oral, but both of them may be socially mal-adjusted and find it difficult to establish

50

contact with their fellow-men. (The classification by types can thus be a source of confusion if we do not realize that types are merely convenient abstractions.

Let us return now to the normal man, who is our standard for measuring variations. The normal man is an individual who lives in society and whose mode of life is so adapted that whether he wants it or not society derives a certain advantage from his work. Also from a psychological point of view he has enough energy and courage to meet the problems and difficulties as they come along. Both of these qualities are missing in the case of psychopathic persons: they are neither socially adjusted nor are they psychologically adjusted to the daily tasks of life. As an illustration we may take the case of a certain individual, a man of thirty who was always at the last moment escaping the solution of his problems. He had a friend but was very suspicious of him, and as a result this friendship never prospered. Friendship cannot grow under such conditions because the other partner feels the tension in the relation. We can readily see how this man really had no friends despite the fact that he was on speaking terms with a large number of persons. He was not sufficiently interested nor adjusted socially to make friends. In fact he did not like society, and was always silent in company. He explained this on the ground that in company he never had any ideas and therefore he had nothing to say.

Moreover, the man was bashful. He had a pink skin which flushed from time to time when he talked. When he could overcome this bashfulness he would speak quite well. What he really needed was to be helped in this direction without criticism. Of course when he was in this state he did not present a nice picture and was not very much liked by his neighbors. He felt this, and as a result his dislike for speech increased. One might say that his style of life was such that if he approached other persons in society he called attention to himself.

Next to social life and the art of getting along with friends, is the question of occupation. Now our patient always had the fear that

51

he might fail in his occupation, and so he studied day and night. He overworked and overstrained himself. And because he overstrained himself he put himself out of commission for solving the question of occupation.

If we compare our patient's approach to the first and second questions in his life, we see that he was always in too great a tension. This is a sign that he had a great feeling of inferiority. He undervalued himself "and looked on others and on new situations as things that were unfriendly to him. He acted as though he was in an enemy country.

We have now enough data to picture the style of life of this man. We can see that he wants to go on but at the same time he is blocked because he fears defeat. It is as if he stood before an abyss, straining and always at a tension. He manages to go forward but only conditionally, and he would prefer to stay at home and not mingle with others.

The third question with which this man was confronted and it is a question on which most persons are not very well prepared is the question of love. He hesitated to approach the other sex. He found that he wanted to love and to get married, but on account of his great feeling of inferiority he was too frightened to face the prospect. He could not accomplish what he wanted and, so we see his whole behavior and attitude summed up in the words, "Yes . . . but!" We see him in love with one girl and then in love with another. This is of course a frequent occurrence with neurotic persons because in a sense two girls are less than one. This truth sometimes accounts for a tendency towards polygamy.

And now let us take up the reasons for this style of life. Individual Psychology undertakes to analyze the causes for a style of life. This man established his style of life during the first four or five years. At that time some tragedy happened which moulded and formed him, and so we have to look for the tragedy. We can see that something made him lose his normal interest in others arid gave him the impression that life is simply one great difficulty and that it

52

is better not to go on at all than to be always confronting difficult situations. Therefore he became cautious, hesitant, and a seeker of ways of escape.

We must mention the fact that he was a first child. We have already spoken about the great significance of this position. We have shown how the chief problem in the case of a first child arises from the fact that he is for years the center of attention, only to be displaced from his glory and another preferred. In a great many cases where a person is bashful and afraid to go on we find the reason to be that another person has been preferred. Hence in this case it is not difficult to find out where the trouble lies.

In many cases we need only ask a patient. Are you the first, second, or third child? Then we have all we need. We can also use an entirely different method: we can ask for old remembrances, which we shall discuss at some length in the next chapter. This method is worthwhile because these remembrances or first pictures are a part of the building up of the early style of life which we have called the prototype. One comes upon an actual part of the prototype when a person tells of his early remembrances. Looking back, everybody remembers certain important things, and indeed what is fixed in memory is always important. There are schools of psychology which act on the opposite assumption. They believe that what a person has forgotten is the most important point, but there is really no great difference between the two ideas. Perhaps a person can tell us his conscious remembrances, but he does not know what they mean. He does not see their connection with his actions. Hence r the result is the same, whether we emphasize the hidden or forgotten significance of conscious memories or the importance of forgotten memories.

Little descriptions of old remembrances are highly illuminating. Thus a man might tell you that when he was small, his mother took him and his younger brother to market. That is enough. We can then discover his style of life. He pictures himself and a younger brother. Therefore we see it must have been important to him to have had a younger brother. Lead him further and you may find a situation similar to a certain one in which a man recalled that it began to rain that day. His mother took him in her arms, but when she saw the younger brother she put him down to carry the little one. Thus we can picture his style of life. He always has the expectation that another person will be preferred. And so we can understand why he cannot speak in society for he is always looking around to see if another will not be preferred. The same is true with friendship. He is always thinking that another is more preferred by his friend, and as a result he can never have a true friend. He is constantly suspicious, looking out for little things that disturb friendship.

We can also see how the tragedy he has experienced has hindered the development of his social interest. He recalls that his mother took the younger brother in her arms and we see that he feels that this baby took more of his mother's attention than he did. He feels that the younger brother is preferred and is looking constantly for confirmation of this idea. He is wholly convinced he is right, and so he is always under strain always under the great difficulty of trying to accomplish things when some one else is preferred. Now the only solution for such a suspicious person is complete isolation, so that he would not have to compete at all with others and would be, so to speak, the only human being on this earth's crust. Sometimes indeed it appears in fancy to such a child that the whole world has broken down, that he is the only person left and that hence no one else can be preferred. We see how he taps all the possibilities to save himself. But he does not go along the lines of logic, common sense, or truth rather along the lines of suspicion. He lives in a limited world, and he has a private idea of escape. He has absolutely no connection with others and no interest in others. But he is not to be blamed for we know that he is not really normal.

It is our task to give such a person the social interest demanded of a well-adjusted human being. How is this to be done? The great difficulty with persons trained in this way is that they are overstrained and are always looking for a confirmation of their fixed ideas. It thus becomes impossible to change their ideas unless somehow we penetrate into their personality in a manner that will disarm their preconceptions. To accomplish this it is necessary to use a certain art and a certain tact. And it is best if the adviser is not closely related or interested in the patient. For if one is directly interested in the case, one will find that one is acting for one's own interest and not for the interest of the patient. The patient will not fail to notice this and will become suspicious.

The important thing is to decrease the patient's feeling of inferiority. It cannot be extirpated altogether, and in fact we do not want to extirpate it because a feeling of inferiority can serve as a useful foundation on which to build. What we have to do is to change the goal. We have seen that his goal has been one of escape just because someone else is preferred, and it is around this complex of ideas that we must work. We must decrease his feeling of inferiority by showing him that he really undervalues himself. We can show him the trouble with his movements and explain to him his tendency to be over-tense, as if standing before a great abyss or as if living in an enemy country and always in danger. We can indicate to him how his fear that others may be preferred, is standing in the way of his doing his best work and making the best spontaneous impression.

If such a person could act as a host in society, making his friends have a good time and being friendly with them and thinking of their interests, he would improve tremendously. But in ordinary social life we see that he does not enjoy himself, does not have ideas and as a result says: "Stupid persons they cannot enjoy me, they cannot interest me."

The trouble with such persons is that they do not understand the situation because of their private intelligence and their lack of common sense.

As we have said, it is as if they were always confronted by enemies and were leading the life of a lone wolf. In the human situation such a life is a tragic abnormality.

Let us now look at another specific case the case of a man afflicted

55

with melancholia. This is a very common illness, but it can be cured. Such persons are distinguishable very early in life. In fact we notice many children who in their approach to a new situation show signs of suffering from melancholia. This melancholy man of whom we are speaking had about ten attacks, and these always occurred when he took a new position. As long as he was in his old position he was nearly normal. But he did not want to go out into society and he wanted to rule others. Consequently he had no friends and at fifty he had not married.

Let us look at his childhood in order to study his style of life. He had been very sensitive and quarrelsome, always ruling his older brothers and sisters by emphasizing his pains and weaknesses. When playing on a couch one day, he pushed them all off. When his aunt reproached him for this, he said, "Now my whole life is ruined because you have blamed me!" And at that time he was only four or five years old.

Such was his style of life always trying to rule others, always complaining of his weakness and of how he suffered. This trait led in his later life to melancholy, which in itself is simply an expression of weakness. Every patient with melancholia uses almost the same words: "My whole life is ruined. I have lost everything." Frequently such a person has been pampered and is so no longer, and this influences his style of life.

Human beings in their reactions to situations are much like the different species of animals. A hare reacts differently to the same situation from a wolf or a tiger. So it is with human individuals. The experiment was once made of taking three different types of boys to a lion's cage in order to see how they would behave on seeing this terrible animal for the first time. The first boy turned and said, "Let's go home." The second boy said, "How nice!" He wanted to appear courageous but he was trembling when he said it. He was a coward. The third boy said, "May I spit at him?" Here then we see three different reactions, three different ways of experiencing the same situation. We see also that for the most part human beings have a tendency to be afraid. '

56

This timidity, when expressed in a social situation, is one of the most frequent causes of maladjustment. There was a man of high-born family who never wanted to exert himself but always wished to be supported. He appeared weak, and of course he could not find a position. Now when the situation at home changed for the worse, his brothers went after him, saying, "You are so stupid that you cannot find a position. You do not understand anything." So this man began to drink. After some months he was a confirmed drunkard and was put in an asylum for two years. It helped him but it did not benefit him permanently, for he was put back into society without preparation. He could find no work except as a laborer, although he was a scion of this well-known family. Soon he began to have hallucinations. He thought a man appeared to tease him so that he could not work. First he could not work because he was a drunkard and then because he had hallucinations. And so we see that it is not the right treatment merely to make a drunkard sober; we must find and correct his style of life.

We discover on investigation that this man was a pampered child, always wanting to be helped. He was not prepared to work alone and we see the results. We must make all children independent, and this can be done only if we get them to understand the mistakes in their style of life. This child should have been trained to do something, and then he would not have had to be ashamed in the presence of his brothers and sisters.

CHAPTER FIVE

OLD REMEMBRANCES

HAVING analyzed the significance of an individual's style of life, we turn now to the topic of old remembrances, which are perhaps the most important means for getting at a style of life. By looking back through childhood memories we are able to uncover the prototype the core of the style of life better than by any other method.

If we want to find out the style of life of a person child or adult we should, after we have heard a little about his complaints, ask him for old remembrances and then compare them with the other facts he has given. For the most part the style of life never changes. There is always the same person with the same personality, the same unity. A style of life, as we have shown, is built up through the striving for a particular goal of superiority, and so we must expect every word, act and feeling to be an organic part of the whole "action line." Now at some points this "action line" is more clearly expressed. This happens particularly in old remembrances.

We should not, however, distinguish too sharply between old and new remembrances, for in new remembrances also the action line is involved. It is easier and more illuminating to find the action line in the beginning, for then we discover the theme and are able to understand how the style of life of a person does not really change. In the style of life formed at the age of four or five we find the connection between remembrances of the past and actions of the present. And so after many observations of this kind we can hold fast to the theory that in these old remembrances we can always find a real part of the patient's prototype.

When a patient looks back into his past we can be sure that anything his memory will turn up will be of emotional interest to him, and thus we will find a clue to his personality. It is not to be denied that the forgotten experiences are also important for the style of life and for the prototype, but many times it is more difficult to find out the forgotten remembrances, or, as they are called, the unconscious remembrances. Both conscious and unconscious remembrances have the common quality of running towards the same goal of superiority. They are both a part of the complete prototype. It is well, therefore, to find both the conscious and unconscious remembrances if possible. Both conscious and unconscious remembrances are in the end about equally important, and the individual himself generally understands neither. It is for the outsider to understand and interpret both of them.

Let us begin with conscious remembrances. Some persons, when they are asked for old remembrances, answer, "I do not know any." We must ask such persons to concentrate and try to remember. After some effort we will find that they will recall something. But this hesitation may be considered as a sign that they do not want to look far back into their childhood and we may then come to the conclusion that their childhood has not been pleasant. We have to lead such people. We must give them hints in order to find out what we want. They always remember something in the end.

Some persons claim that they can remember back to their first year. This is scarcely possible, and the truth is probably that these are fancied memories, not true remembrances. But it does not matter whether they are fancied or true since they are parts of one's personality. Some persons insist that they are not sure whether they remember a thing or whether their parents have told them about it. This, too, is not really important because even if their parents did tell them they have fixed it in their minds and therefore it helps to tell us where their interest lies.

As we have explained in the last chapter it is convenient for certain purposes to classify individuals into types. Now old remembrances go according to types and reveal what is to be expected of the behavior of a particular type. For instance, let us take the case of a person who remembers that he saw a marvelous Christmas tree, filled with lights, presents and holiday cakes. What is the most

59

interesting thing in this story? That he saw. Why does he tell us that he has seen? Because he is always interested in visual things. He has struggled against some difficulties in sight, and, having been trained, has always been interested and attentive to seeing. Perhaps this is not the most important element of his style of life, but it is an interesting and important part. It indicates that if we are to give him an occupation it should be one in which he will use his eyes.

In school the education of children too often disregards this principle of types. We may find a child interested in sight who will not listen because he always wants to be looking at something. In the case of such a child we ought to be patient in trying to educate him to hear. Many children at school are taught only in one way because they enjoy with one sense. They may be only good at listening or good at seeing. Some always like to be moving and to be working. We cannot expect the same results for the three types of children, especially if the teacher prefers one method, as, for example the method for listening children. When such a method is used the lookers and the doers will suffer and will be hindered in their development.

Consider the case of a young man, twenty-four years old, who suffered from fainting spells. When asked for his remembrances, he recalled that when he was four years old he fainted when he heard an engine whistle. In other words, he was a man who had heard, and was therefore interested in hearing. It is not necessary to explain here how this young man later developed fainting spells, but it is sufficient to note that from his childhood he was very sensitive to sounds. He was very musical, for he could not bear noises, disharmonies or strident tones. We are not surprised, therefore, that he should have been so affected by the sound of a whistle. There are often things in which children or adults are interested because they have suffered through them. The reader will remember the case of the man with asthma mentioned in a previous chapter. He had been bound tightly about his lungs in childhood for some trouble, and as a result had developed an extraordinary interest in ways to breathe.

One meets persons whose whole interest seems to lie in things to eat. Their early remembrances have to do with eating. It seems the most important thing in the world for them how to eat, what to eat, and what not to eat. We will often find that difficulties connected with eating in early life have enhanced the importance of eating for such an individual.

We turn now to a case of remembrance that has to do with movement and walking. We have seen how many children cannot move very well at the beginning of life because they are weak or suffer from rickets. They become abnormally interested in movement and always want to hurry. The case is an illustration of this fact. A man of fifty came to a doctor complaining that whenever he accompanied a person across the street he suffered from a terrible fear that they would both be run over. When alone he was never bothered with this fear, and in fact was very composed in crossing the street. It was only when another was with him that he wanted to save this person. He would then grasp his companion's arm, push him now right and now left, and generally annoy him. We meet with such persons occasionally, though not frequently. Let us analyze the reasons for his stupid actions.

Asked for his old remembrances, he explained that when he was three years old he could not move very well and was suffering from rickets. He was twice run over when crossing a street. And so, now that he was a man it was important for him to prove that he had overcome this weakness. He wanted to show, so to speak, that he was the only man who could cross a street. He was always looking for an opportunity to prove it whenever he was with a companion. Of course to be able to cross a street safely is not something that most people would take pride in or compete with others. But with such persons as our patient, the desire to move and to show off about the ability to move can be quite lively.

We turn now to another case the case of a boy who was on the way to becoming a criminal. He stole, played "hookey" from school, etc. until his parents were in despair. His early remembrances were of how he had always wanted to move around and to hurry. He was

61

now working with his father and was sitting still all day. From the nature of the case part of the treatment prescribed was that he be made a salesman a traveller for his father's business.

One of the most significant types of old remembrances is the memory of a death during the period of childhood. When children see a person die suddenly and abruptly, the effect on their minds is very marked. Sometimes such children become morbid. Sometimes, without becoming morbid, they devote their whole lives to the problem of death and are always occupied in struggling against illness and death in some form. We may find many of these children interested in medicine later in life, and they may become physicians or chemists. Such a goal of course is on the useful side of life. They not only struggle against death but help others to do so. Sometimes, however, the prototype develops a very egotistical point of view. A child who was very much affected by the death of an older sister was asked what he wanted to be. The answer expected was that he would be a physician; instead he replied: "A grave-digger." He was asked why he wanted to follow this occupation, and he answered, "Because I want to be the one to bury the others and not the one buried." This goal, we see, is on the useless side of life, for the boy is interested only in himself.

Let us turn now to consider old remembrances of people who were pampered children. The old remembrances mirror the characteristics of this class very clearly. A child of this type often mentions his mother. Now perhaps this is natural but it is a sign that he has had to struggle for a favorable situation. Sometimes the old remembrances seem to be quite innocuous, but they repay analysis. For instance, a man tells you, "I was sitting in my room and my mother stood by the cabinet," This appears unimportant, but his mentioning his mother is a sign that this has been a matter of interest to him. Sometimes the mother is more hidden and the study more complicated. We have to guess about the mother. Thus the man in question may tell you, "I remember I made a trip." If you ask who accompanied him, you will discover it was his mother. Or, if children tell us, "I remember I was in the country at a certain place one summer," we can presuppose that the father was in the city working and the mother was with the children. We can ask, "Who was with you?" In this way we often see the hidden influence of the mother.

From a study of these remembrances we can see a struggle for preferment. We can see how a child in the course of his development begins to value the pampering his mother gives him. This is important for our understanding because if children or adults tell us about such remembrances, we may be sure that such persons always feel that they are in danger or that another will be preferred to them. We see the tension becoming increased and more and more obvious and we see that their minds are sharply focussed on this idea. Such a fact is important: it indicates that in later life such persons will be jealous.

Sometimes persons express interest on one point above all others. For instance a child may say, "I had to watch my little sister one day and I wanted to protect her very well. I put her at the table but the cover caught and my little sister fell down." This child was only four years old. It is of course an early age at which to permit an older child to watch a younger girl. We can see what a tragedy it is in the life of the older child who was doing everything possible to protect the younger one. This particular older girl grew up and married a kind we might almost say, obedient husband. But she was always jealous and critical, always afraid that her husband would prefer another. We can easily understand how the husband tired of her and turned to the children.

Sometimes tension is more clearly expressed and people remember that they actually wanted to hurt other members of their family, in fact to kill them. Such persons are people who are interested in their own affairs exclusively. They do not like other people. They feel a certain rivalry towards them. This feeling already exists in the prototype.

We have here the type of person who can never finish anything because he fears someone else will be preferred in friendship and comradeship, or because he is suspicious of people always trying to surpass him. He can never really become a part of society because of the idea that another might outshine him and be preferred. In every occupation he is extremely tense. This attitude appears specially in connection with love and marriage.

Even if we cannot completely cure such persons, we can, with a certain art in the study of old remembrances, see that they improve.

One of the subjects for our methods of treatment was the boy whom we described in another chapter as having gone to market with his mother and younger brother one day. When it started to rain the mother took him up in her arms, but, on noticing the younger brother, she set him down and took up the younger child. Hence he felt that the younger brother was preferred.

If we can obtain such old remembrances we can predict, as we have said, what will happen later in the life of our patients. However, it must be remembered that old remembrances are not reasons, they are hints. They are signs of what happened and how development took place. They indicate the movement toward a goal and what obstacles had to be overcome. They show how a person becomes more interested in one side of life than another. We see that he may have what we call a trauma, along the lines of sex, for instance; that is, he may be more interested in such matters than in others. We cannot be surprised if, when we ask for old remembrances, we hear some sex experiences. Some persons are interested in sex features more than in others at an early age. It is part of the usual human behavior to be interested in sex but, as I have said before, there are many varieties and degrees of interest. We often find that in a case where a person tells us about sex remembrances, he later develops in this direction. The resulting life is not harmonious because this one side of human life is over-valued. There are persons who insist that everything has a sex basis. On the other hand, there are others who insist that the stomach is the most important organ and we will find that old remembrances parallel later characteristics in such instances also.

64

There was a boy whose getting into high school was always a riddle. He wanted to be constantly moving, and would never settle down to study. He was always thinking about something else, frequenting coffee houses and visiting at friends' houses all when he should have been studying. It was therefore interesting to examine his old remembrances. He said, "I can remember lying in my cradle and looking at the wall. I noticed the paper on the wall, with all its flowers, figures, etc." This person was prepared only for lying in a cradle, not for taking examinations. He could not concentrate on his studies because he was always thinking of other things and trying to go after two hares at once, which cannot be done. We can see that this man was a pampered child and could not work alone.

We come now to the hated child. This type is rare and represents extreme cases. If a child is really hated from the beginning of life, he cannot live. Such a child would perish. Usually children have parents or a nurse who pampers them to some extent and satisfies their desires. We find the hated children among illegitimate, criminal and not wanted children, and we often see these children becoming depressed. Frequently we find in their remembrances this feeling of being hated. For instance, there was the case of a man who said, "I remember I was spanked; my mother scolded me, criticised me until I ran away." While running away he came very nearly being drowned.

This man came to a psychologist because he could not leave his home. We see from his old remembrances that he went out once and met with great danger. This stuck in his memory and he constantly looked for danger when he went out. He was a bright child but always feared that he might not make first place in examinations. So he hesitated and could not go on. When he at last got to the university he feared that he could not compete in the prescribed way. We see how all this may be traced back to his old remembrances of danger.

Another case which may be taken as an illustration is that of an orphan whose parents died when he was only about a year old. He

65

had rickets, and, being in an asylum, he was not cared for properly. Nobody looked after him, and in later life it was very difficult for him to make friends or comrades. Looking back to his remembrances we see that he always felt that others were preferred. This feeling played an important part in his development. He always felt hated and this hindered his approach to all problems. He was excluded from all questions and situations of life, such as love, marriage, friendship, business all these situations which required contact with his fellows on account of his feeling of inferiority.

Another interesting case is that of a middle-aged man who was always complaining of sleeplessness. He was 46 or 48 years old, married, and had children. He was very critical of everybody, and was always trying to tyrannize, particularly over the members of his family. His actions made everyone feel miserable.

When asked for his old remembrances he explained that he had grown up in a home with quarrelsome parents, who were always fighting and threatening each other, so that he was afraid of them both. He went to school dirty and uncared for. One day his usual teacher was absent and a substitute took her place. This substitute woman was interested in her task and its possibilities. She saw that it was a good and noble work. She saw possibilities in this ill-kept boy and went out to encourage him. This was the first time in his life he had had any such treatment. From that time on he began to develop, but it was always as if he were pushed from behind. He did not really believe he was able to be superior, and so he worked all day and half the night. In this way he grew up trained to use half the night for his work or else not to sleep at all but to spend the time thinking of what he had to do. As a result he grew to think that it was necessary to be awake almost all night in order to accomplish results.

We see later his desire to be superior expressed in his attitude towards his family and in his behavior towards others. His family being weaker than he, he could appear in the role of a conqueror

66

before them. His wife and children suffered through this type of behavior, as was inevitable.

Summing up the character of this man as a whole, we may say that he had a goal of superiority and that it was the goal of a person with a great feeling of inferiority. This we often find among over-strained persons. Their tenseness is a sign of their doubt of their own success, and their doubt in turn is covered up by a superiority complex which is really a superiority pose. A study of old remembrances reveals the situation in its true light.

CHAPTER SIX

ATTITUDES AND MOVEMENTS

IN the last chapter we endeavoured to describe the manner in which old remembrances and fancies may be used to illuminate the hidden style of life of an individual. Now the study of old remembrances is only one device of a whole class of devices for the study of personality. They all depend on the principle of using isolated parts for an interpretation of the whole. Besides old remembrances we can observe movements and attitudes. The movements themselves are expressed or imbedded in attitudes, and the attitudes are an expression of that whole attitude to life which constitutes what we call the style of life.

Let us first speak about the movements of the body. Everybody knows that we judge a person by his manner of standing, walking, moving, expressing himself, etc. We do not always consciously judge, but there is always a feeling of sympathy or antipathy created by these impressions.

Let us consider attitudes in standing, for instance. We notice promptly whether a child or adult stands upright or whether he is crooked or bent. This is not very difficult. We have to watch specially for exaggerations. A person who stands too straight, in a stretched position, causes us to suspect that he is using too much power to assume this posture. We can suppose that this person feels much less great than he wants to appear. In this little point we can see how he mirrors what we have called the superiority complex. He wants to appear more courageous he wants to express himself more as he would be if he were not so tense.

On the other hand we see persons with just the opposite posture persons who appear bent and who are always stooping. Such a posture implies to a certain extent that they are cowards. But it is a rule of our art and science that we should always be cautious,

68

looking for other points and never judging solely by one consideration. Sometimes we feel that we are almost sure of being correct, but we still want to verify our judgment by other points. We ask, "Are we right in insisting that persons who stoop are always cowards? What can we expect of them in a difficult situation?"

To look at another point in this connection, we will notice how such a person always tries to rest upon something, to lean on a table or chair for instance. He does not trust his own power but wants to be supported. This reflects the same attitude of mind as when standing crooked, and so when we find both types of action present our judgment is somewhat confirmed.

We will find that children who want always to be supported have not the same posture as independent children. We can tell the degree of independence by how a child stands, how he approaches other persons. In such cases we need not be in doubt, for we have many possibilities of confirming our conclusion. And once we have confirmed our conclusion, we can take steps to remedy the situation and put the child on the right path.

Thus we may experiment with such a child who wants to be supported. Sit his mother on a chair and then let the child come into the room. We will find that he does not look at any other person but goes directly towards his mother and leans on the chair or against his mother. This confirms what we expect that the child wants to be supported.

It is interesting also to note the child's approach, for it shows the degree of social interest and adjustment. It expresses the confidence of the child in others. We will find that a person who does not want to approach others and who always stands far away is also reserved in other respects. We will find that he does not speak enough and is unusually silent.

We can see how all these things point the same way because every human being is a unity and reacts as such towards the questions of life. As an illustration let us take the case of a woman who came to a doctor for treatment. The doctor expected that she would take a seat near him, but when she was offered a chair she looked around and took a seat far away. It could only be concluded that this was a person who wanted to be connected with only one person. She said that she was married, and from this the whole story could be guessed. It could be guessed that she wanted to be connected only with her husband. It could also be guessed that she wanted to be pampered, that she is the sort of person who would demand that her husband be very exact and always on time in coming home. If she was alone she would suffer great anxiety, and she would never want to go out of her house alone and would not enjoy meeting other people. In short from her one physical movement we could guess the whole story. But we have also ways of confirming our theory.

She may tell us: "I am suffering from anxiety." Now nobody would understand what this meant unless he knew that anxiety can be used as a weapon to rule another person. If a person or adult suffers from anxiety we can guess that there is another person who supports this child or adult.

There was once a couple who insisted that they were free thinkers. Such people believe that everybody can do what he wants in marriage, so long as each one tells the other what happens. The consequence was that the husband had some love affairs and told all of them to his wife. She seemed perfectly content. But later on she began to suffer from anxiety. She would not go out alone. Her husband must always go with her. We can see then how this free thinking became modified by anxiety or phobia.

Some persons will always stay near a wall of a house and lean on it. This is a sign that they are not courageous enough, not independent enough. Let us analyze the prototype of such a timid and hesitating person. There was a boy who came to school appearing very shy. This is an important sign that he does not want to be connected with others. He had no friends and was always waiting for school

70

to close. He moved very slowly, and would go down the stairs close to the wall, look down the street and rush for his house. He was not a good pupil in school, and in fact was very poor in his school work since he did not feel happy inside of school walls. He always wanted to go home to his mother, a widow who was weak and pampered him very much.

In order to understand more about the case the doctor went to talk with his mother. He asked her, "Does he want to go to bed?" She said, "Yes." "Does he cry out at night?" "No." "Does he wet the bed?" "No."

The doctor thought that either he had made a mistake or that the boy had made a mistake. Then he concluded that the boy must sleep in bed with his mother. How was this conclusion arrived at? Well, to cry out at night is to demand attention of the mother. If he slept in her bed, this would not be necessary. Similarly to wet the bed is also to demand the mother's attention. The doctor's conclusion was verified: the boy slept in bed with his mother.

If we look carefully we will see that all the little things to which the psychologist pays attention form part of a consistent plan of life. Hence when we can see the goal in the child's case, to be always tied up with his mother we can conclude a great many things. We can conclude by this means whether a child is feebleminded or not, A feeble-minded child would not be able to establish such an intelligent plan of life.

Now let us turn to the mental attitudes distinguishable in persons. Some persons are more or less pugnacious. Some on the other hand want to give up the ship. However, we never see a person who really gives up. It is not possible, for it is beyond human nature. The normal being cannot give up. If he seems to do so, it indicates even more of a struggle to carry on than otherwise.

There is a type of child who always wants to give up. He is usually the center of attention in a family. Everybody has to care for him, push him forward and admonish him. He must be supported in life

71

and is always a burden to others. This is his goal of superiority he expresses his desire to dominate others in this fashion. Such a goal of superiority is of course the result of an inferiority complex, as we have already shown. If he had not been doubtful of his own powers, he would not take this easy way out for attaining success.

There was a boy of 17 who illustrated this trait. He was the oldest in the family. We have already seen how the oldest child usually experiences a tragedy when the coming of another child dethrones him from his place in the center of family affections. This was the case with this boy. He was very depressed and peevish and had no occupation. One day he tried to commit suicide. Soon after that he came to a doctor and explained that he had had a dream before his attempt at suicide. He dreamt he had shot his father. We see how such a person depressed, lazy and not moving has all the time the possibility of movement present in his mind. We also see how all these children who are indolent in school, and all these indolent adults who seem incapable of doing anything may be on the brink of danger. Oftentimes this indolence is only on the surface. Then something happens, and we have an attempt at suicide, or else a neurotic condition or insanity may appear. To ascertain the mental attitude of such persons is sometimes a difficult scientific task.

Shyness in a child is another thing that is full of danger. A shy child must be carefully treated. The shyness must be corrected or it will ruin his whole life. He will always have great difficulties unless his shyness is corrected, for in our culture things are so established that only courageous persons get good results and the advantages of life. If a person is courageous and suffers defeat he is not hurt so much, but a shy person makes his escape to the useless side of life as soon as he sees difficulties ahead. Such children will become neurotics or insane in later life.

We see such persons going about with a hangdog air, and when they are with others they stammer and will not speak or they will avoid people altogether.

The characteristics that we have been describing are mental

attitudes. They are not inborn or inherited, but are simply reactions toward a situation. A given characteristic is the answer that my style of life gives to my apperception of a problem that confronts me. Of course it is not always the logical answer that the philosopher would expect. It is the answer that my childhood experiences and mistakes have trained me to make.

We can see the functioning of these attitudes as well as the way in which they have been built up in children or in abnormal persons better than we can in the case of normal adults. The prototype stage of the style of life, as we have seen, is much clearer and simpler than the later style. In fact one may compare the functioning of the prototype to an unripe fruit that will assimilate everything that comes along manure, water, food, air. All these things will be taken up in its development. The difference between a prototype and the style of life is like the difference between an unripe and a ripe fruit. The unripe fruit stage in human beings is much easier to open up and examine, but what it reveals is to a large extent valid for the ripe fruit stage.

We can see, for example, how a child who is a coward at the beginning of life expresses this cowardice in all his attitudes. A world of differences separate the cowardly child from the aggressive, fighting child. The fighting child always has a certain degree of courage which is the natural outgrowth of what we have called common sense. Sometimes, however, a very cowardly child may appear like a hero in a certain situation. This happens whenever he is deliberately trying to attain first place. This is clearly illustrated in the case of a boy who did not know how to swim. One day he went swimming with other boys who had asked him to join them. The water was very deep, and the boy, who could not swim, nearly drowned. This of course is not real courage, and is all on the useless side of life. The boy merely did what he did because he wanted to be admired. He ignored the danger he was in, and hoped that the others would save him.

The question of courage and timidity is psychologically closely related to the belief in predestination. The belief in predestination affects our capacity for useful action. There are persons who have such a feeling of superiority that they feel they can accomplish anything. They know everything and do not want to learn anything. We all know the result of such ideas. Children who feel this way in school usually get poor marks. There are other people who always want to try the most dangerous things: they feel that nothing can happen to them, that they cannot suffer defeat. Very often the result is a bad one.

We find this feeling of predestination among people whenever something terrible has happened in their lives and they have remained unhurt. For instance, they may have been present in a serious accident and were not killed. As a result they feel that they are destined for higher purposes. There was once a man who had such a feeling but after going through an experience which resulted differently from his expectation he lost courage and became depressed and melancholy. His most important support had fallen away.

When asked for his early remembrances he related a very significant experience. He said he was once about to go to a theatre in Vienna, but had to attend to something first. When he finally arrived at the theatre it had burned down. Everything was over, but he was saved. One can well understand how such a person felt himself destined for higher things. All went well until he suffered defeat in his relations with his wife. Then he broke down.

Much could be said and written about the significance of the belief in fatalism. It affects whole peoples and civilizations as well as individuals, but for our part we desire to point out only its connection with the springs of psychological activity and the style of life. The belief in predestination is in many ways a cowardly escape from the task of striving and building up activity along the useful line. For that reason it will prove a false support.

One of the basic attitudes of mind that affects our relations with our fellow-men is the attitude of envy. Now to be envious is a sign of inferiority. True, we all have a certain amount of envy in our make-

74

up. A small amount does no harm and is quite common. We must, however, demand that envy be useful. It must result in work, in a going on, and in a facing of problems. In such cases it is not useless. For that reason we should pardon the bit of envy which is found in all of us.

On the other hand jealousy is a much more difficult and dangerous mental attitude, because it cannot be made useful. There is no single way in which a jealous person can be useful.

Moreover, we see in jealousy the result of a great and deep feeling of inferiority. A jealous person is afraid of his inability to hold his or her partner. And so at the very moment when he wants to influence his partner in some manner, he betrays his weakness by his expressions of jealousy. If we look in the prototype of such a person we shall see a sense of curtailment. In fact whenever we meet with jealous persons it is well to look back into their past and see whether we have not to do with a dethroned person who expects that he will be dethroned again.

From the general problem of envy and jealousy we may pass to the consideration of a very peculiar type of envy the envy on the part of the female sex of the superior social position of the male sex. We find many women and girls who want to be boys. This attitude is quite understandable, for if we look at things impartially we can see that in our culture the men are always in the lead; they are always more appreciated, valued and esteemed than women. Morally this is not right and ought to be corrected. Now girls see that in the family the men and boys are much more comfortable and do not have to bother with little things. They see that they are freer in many ways, and this superior freedom of the male sex makes them dissatisfied with their own role. They therefore try to act like boys. This imitation of boys may appear in various ways. We see them, for instance, trying to dress like boys, and in this they are sometimes supported by their parents since boys* clothes are admittedly more comfortable. Now a number of these acts are useful and need not be discouraged. But there are some useless attitudes, as when a girl wants to be called by a boy's name and not by the name of a girl. Such girls get very angry if others do not call them by the boy's name which they have chosen. This attitude is very dangerous if it reflects something below the surface and is not a mere prank. In such a case it may appear later in life as a dissatisfaction with the sex role and a distaste for marriage or, when married, a distaste for the sex role of woman.

One should not find fault with women for wearing short clothes, because it is an advantage. It is also fitting for them to develop like men in many ways, and to have a job like men. But it is dangerous for them to be dissatisfied with their feminine role and try to adopt the vices of men.

This dangerous tendency makes its appearance in the adolescent period, for it is then that the prototype becomes poisoned. The immature minds of the girls become jealous of the privileges of the boys. It reacts in the desire to imitate boys. Now this is a superiority complex it is an escape from proper development.

As we have said, this can lead to a great disinclination for love and marriage. This is not to say that girls who have this disinclination do not want to be married, for in our culture not to be married is taken as a sign of defeat. Even the girls who are not interested in marriage want to get married.

One who believes in regulating the basis of the relations of the sexes on the principle of equality should not encourage this "masculine protest" of women. The equality of the sexes must be fitted into the natural scheme of things, while the masculine protest is a blind revolt against reality and is thus a superiority complex. As a matter of fact through this masculine protest all the sex functions can be disturbed and affected. Many serious symptoms can be produced, and if we trace them back we shall see that the conditions started in childhood.

Not so frequently as in the case of girls who want to be boys, we also meet with the boy who wants to be like a girl. He wants to imitate not the ordinary girl, but the type of girl who flirts in an exaggerated manner. Such boys use face powder, they wear flowers, and try to act in the manner of a frivolous girl. This is also a form of superiority complex.

We find in fact that in many such cases the boy had grown up in an environment in which a woman was at the head. Thus the boy grew up to imitate the traits of the mother, not of the father.

There was a boy who came for consultation because of certain sex troubles. He related how he was always with his mother. The father was almost a nonentity in the home. Now his mother had been a dressmaker before she was married and continued something of her occupation after her marriage. The boy being always near her got to be interested in the things she made. He began to sew and draw pictures of dresses for women, etc. One can judge how interested he was in his mother from the fact that at four years he had learned to tell time because his mother always went out at four and came back at five o'clock. Impelled by his pleasure on seeing her return, he learned to read the clock.

Later in life, when he went to school, he acted like a girl. He took no part in sports or games. The boys made fun of him, and at times they even kissed him, as they frequently do in such cases. One day they had to give a theatrical play, and as we can imagine this boy had the part of a girl. He acted it so well that many in the audience actually thought he was a girl. One man in the audience even fell in love with him. In this way this boy got to see that even if he could not be much appreciated as a man he could be greatly appreciated as a woman. This was the genesis of his later sexual troubles.

CHAPTER SEVEN

DREAMS AND THEIR INTERPRETATION

FOR Individual Psychology consciousness and unconsciousness form a single unity, as we have already explained in a number of contexts. In the last two chapters we have been interpreting conscious parts remembrances, attitudes, movements in terms of the individual whole. We shall now apply the same method of interpretation to our unconscious or semiconscious life the life of our dreams. The justification for this method is that our dream life is just as much a part of the whole, as our waking life no more and no less. Followers of other schools of psychology are constantly trying to find new views concerning dreams, but our understanding of dreams has been developed along the same line as our understanding of all the integral parts manifested in the expressions and movements of the psyche.

Now just as our waking life, we have seen, is determined by the goal of superiority, so we may see that dreams are determined by the individual goal of superiority. A dream is always a part of the style of life and we always find the prototype involved in it. In fact it is only when you see how the prototype is bound up to a particular dream that you can be sure that you have really understood the dream. Also, if you know a person well, you can pretty nearly guess the character of his dreams.

Take, for instance, our knowledge that mankind as a whole is really cowardly. From this general fact we can presuppose that the largest number of dreams will be dreams of fear, danger, or anxiety. And so if we know a person and see that his goal is to escape the solution of life's problems, we can guess that he often dreams that he falls down. Such a dream is like a warning to him: "Do not go on you will be defeated." He expresses his view of the future in this way by falling. The large majority of men have these dreams of falling.

78

A specific case is a student on the eve of an examination a student whom we know to be a quitter. We can guess what will happen with him. He is worried the whole day, cannot concentrate, and finally says to himself, "The time is too short." He wants to postpone the examination. His dream will be one of falling down. And this expresses his style of life, for to attain his goal, he must dream in such a way.

Take another student who makes progress in his studies, is courageous and not afraid, and never uses subterfuges. We can also guess his dreams. Before an examination he will dream that he climbs a high mountain, is enchanted with the view from the mountain top, and in this way awakes. This is an expression of his current of life, and we can see how it reflects his goal of accomplishment.

Then there is the person who is limited the person who can proceed only up to a certain point. Such a person dreams about limits, and about being unable to escape persons and difficulties. He often has dreams of being chased and hunted.

Before we go on to the next type of dream it may be well to remark that the psychologist is never discouraged if somebody says to him, "I will not tell you any dreams for I cannot remember them. But I will make up some dreams." The psychologist knows that his fancy cannot create anything other than that which his style of life commands. His made-up dreams are just as good as his genuinely remembered dreams, for his imagination and fancy will also be an expression of his style of life.

Fancy need not literally copy a man's real movements in order to be an expression of his style of life. We find, for example, the type of person who lives more in fancies than in reality. He is the type that is very cowardly in the daytime but quite courageous in dreams. But we will always find some manifestations which indicate that he does not want to finish his work. Such manifestations will be quite evident even in his courageous dreams.

It is always the purpose of a dream to pave the way towards the goal of superiority that is to say, the individual's private goal of superiority. All the symptoms, movements and dreams of a person are a form of training to enable one to find this dominating goal be the goal one of being the center of attention, of domineering, or of escape.

The purpose of a dream is neither logically nor truthfully expressed. It exists in order to create a certain feeling, mood or emotion, and it is impossible fully to unravel its obscurities. But in this it differs from waking life and the movements of waking life only in degree, not in kind. We have seen that the answers of the psyche to life's problems are relative to the individual scheme of life: they do not fit into a preestablished frame of logic, although it is our aim, for purposes of social intercourse, to make them do so more and more. Now once we give up the absolute point of view for waking life, dream life loses its mystery. It becomes a further expression of the same relativity and the same mixture of fact and emotion that we find in waking life.

Historically dreams have always appeared very mysterious to primitive peoples, and they have generally resorted to the prophetic interpretation. Dreams were regarded as prophecies of events to come. In this there was a half-truth. It is true that a dream is a bridge that connects the problem which confronts the dreamer with his goal of attainment. In this way a dream will often come true, because the dreamer will be training his part during the dream and will be thus preparing for it to come true.

Another way of saying the same thing is that there is the same interconnectedness revealed in dreams as in our waking life. If a person is keen and intelligent he can foresee the future whether he analyzes his waking life or his dream life. What he does is to diagnose. For example if somebody dreams that an acquaintance has died and the person does die, this might be no more than what a physician or a close relative could foresee. What the dreamer does is to think in his sleep rather than in waking life.

80

The prophetic view of dreams, precisely because it contains a certain half-truth, is a superstition. It is generally clung to by persons who believe in other superstitions. Or else it is championed by men who seek importance by giving the impression that they are prophets.

To dispel the prophetic superstition and the mystery that surrounds dreams we have to explain of course why most people do not understand their own dreams. The explanation is to be found in the fact that few people know themselves even in waking life. Few persons have the power of reflective self -analysis which permits them to see whither they are headed, and the analysis of dreams is, as we have said, a more complicated and obscure affair than the analysis of waking behavior. It is thus no wonder that the analysis of dreams should be beyond the scope of most persons and it is also no wonder that in their ignorance of what is involved they should turn to charlatans.

It will help us to understand the logic of dreams if we compare it, not directly with the movements of normal waking life, but with the type of phenomena which we have described in previous chapters as a manifestation of private intelligence. The reader will remember how we described the attitudes of criminals, problem children and neurotics how they create a certain feeling, temper or mood in order to convince themselves of a given fact. Thus the murderer justifies himself by saying, "Life has no place for this man; therefore I must kill him." By emphasizing in his own mind the view that there is not sufficient place on earth he creates a certain feeling which prepares him for the murder.

Such a person may also reason that so-and-so has nice trousers and he has not. He puts such value on this circumstance that he becomes envious. His goal of superiority becomes to have nice trousers, and so we may find him dreaming a dream which creates a certain emotion which will lead to the accomplishment of that goal. We see this illustrated, in fact, in well-known dreams. There are, for instance, the dreams of Joseph in the Bible. He dreamt that all the others bent before him. Now we can see how this dream

81

fitted in with the whole episode of the coat of many colors and with his banishment by his brothers.

Another well-known dream is that of the Greek poet Simonides, who was invited to go to Asia Minor to lecture. He hesitated and continually postponed the trip in spite of the fact that the ship was in the harbor waiting for him. His friends tried to make him go, but to no avail. Then he had a dream. He dreamt that a dead man whom he had once found in a forest appeared to him and said, "Because you were so pious and cared for me in the forest, I now warn you not to go to Asia Minor." Simonides arose and said, "I will not go." But he had already been inclined not to go before he ever had the dream. He had simply created a certain feeling or emotion to back up a conclusion that he had already reached, although he did not understand his own dream.

If one understands it is clear that one creates a certain fantasy for purposes of self-deception, which results in a desired feeling or emotion. Frequently this is all that is remembered of the dream.

In considering this dream of Simonides we come to another point. What should be the procedure in interpreting dreams. Firstly, we must bear in mind that a dream is part of a person's creative power. Simonides, dreaming, used his fancy and built up a sequence. He selected the incident of the dead man. Why should this poet pick the experience of the dead man from out of all his experiences? Obviously because he was very much concerned with ideas of death, due to the fact that he was terrified at the thought of sailing on a ship. In those days a sea voyage presented real danger, and so he hesitated. It is a sign that he was probably not only afraid of seasickness but also that he feared the ship might sink. As a result of this preoccupation with the thought of death, his dream selected the episode of the dead man.

If we consider dreams in this manner, the task of interpretation does not become too difficult. We should remember that the selection of pictures, remembrances and fancies is an indication of the direction in which the mind is moving. It shows you the

82

dreamer's tendency, and eventually we can see the goal at which he wants to arrive.

Let us consider, for example, the dream of a certain married man. He was not content with his family life. He had two children, but was always worried, thinking that his wife did not take care of them and was too much interested in other things. He was always criticising his wife about these things and tried to reform her. One night he dreamt that he had a third child. This child got lost and was not to be found. He reproached his wife because she had not taken care of him.

Here we see his tendency : he had in mind the thought that one of his two children might get lost, but he was not courageous enough to make it one of them in his dream. And so he invented a third child and made him get lost.

Another point to be observed is that he liked his children and did not want them to get lost. Also that he felt that his wife was overburdened with two children and could not care for three. This third child would perish. Hence we find another aspect of the dream, which, when interpreted, reads: "Should I have a third child or not?"

The real result of the dream was that he had created an emotion against his wife. No child really got lost, but he got up in the morning criticising and feeling antagonistic towards her. Thus people frequently get up in the morning argumentative and critical as a result of an emotion created by the night's dream. It is like a state of intoxication and not unlike what one finds in melancholia, where the patient intoxicates himself with ideas of defeat, of death and of all being lost.

We may also see that this man selected things in which he was sure to be superior, as, for instance, the feeling, "I am careful of the children, but my wife is not and therefore one got lost." Thus his tendency to dominate is revealed in his dream.

The modern interpretation of dreams is about twenty-five years old.

83

Dreams were first regarded by Freud as the fulfillment of infantile sex desires. We cannot agree with this, inasmuch as if dreams are such a fulfillment then everything can be expressed in terms of a fulfillment. Every idea behaves in this way going from the depths of the subconscious up into consciousness. The formula of sex-fulfillment thus explains nothing in particular.

Later Freud suggested that the desire for death was involved. But it is certain that this last dream could not be explained very well in this way, for we cannot say that the father wanted the child to get lost and die.

The truth is that there is no specific formula which will explain dreams, except the general postulates which we have discussed about the unity of psychical life and about the special affective character of dream life. This affective character, and its accompaniment of self-deception is a theme with many variations. Thus it is expressed in the preoccupation with comparisons and metaphors. The use of comparisons is one of the best means of deceiving oneself and others. For we may be sure that if a person uses comparisons he does not feel sure that he can convince you with reality and logic. He always wants to influence you by means of useless and far-fetched comparisons.

Even poets deceive, but pleasantly, and we enjoy being entertained by their metaphors and poetic comparisons. We may be sure, however, that they are meant to influence us more than we would be influenced by usual words. If Homer, for example, speaks of an army of Greek soldiers overrunning a field like lions, the metaphor will not deceive us when we think sharply but it will certainly intoxicate us when we are in a poetic mood. The author makes us believe he has marvelous power. He could not do this if he were merely to describe the clothes the soldiers wore and the arms they carried, etc.

We see the same thing in the case of a person who is in difficulty about explaining things: if he sees he cannot convince you, he will use comparisons. This use of comparisons, as we have said, is self-deceptive, and this is the reason it is so prominently manifested in dreams in the selection of pictures, images, etc. This is an artistic way of intoxicating oneself.

The fact that dreams are emotionally intoxicating offers, curiously enough, a method for preventing dreams. If a person understands what he has been dreaming about and realizes that he has been intoxicating himself, he will stop dreaming. To dream will have no more purpose for him. At least this is the case with the present writer, who stopped dreaming as soon as he realized what dreaming meant.

Incidentally it may be said that this realization, to be effective, must have the aspects of a thorough-going emotional conversion. This was brought about, in the case of the writer, by his last dream. The dream occurred during war time. In connection with his duties he was making a great effort to keep a certain man from being sent to the front in a place of danger. In the dream the idea came to him that he had murdered someone, but he did not know whom. He got himself into a bad state wondering, "Whom have I murdered?" The fact is he was simply intoxicated with the idea of making the greatest possible effort to put the soldier in the most favorable position for avoiding death. The dream emotion was meant to be conducive to this idea, but when he understood the subterfuge of the dream, he gave up dreaming altogether, since he did not need to deceive himself in order to do the things that for reasons of logic he might want either to do or to leave undone.

What we have said may be taken as an answer to the question that is frequently asked, "Why do some persons never dream?" These are persons who do not want to deceive themselves. They are too much tied up with movement and logic, and want to face problems. Persons of this sort, if they dream, often forget their dreams very soon. They forget so quickly that they believe they have not dreamed.

This brings up the theory that we always dream and that we forget most of our dreams. If we accepted such a theory it would put a different construction on the fact that some persons never dream: they would then become persons who dream but who always forget their dreams. The present writer does not accept this theory. He rather believes that there are persons who never dream and that there are also dreamers who sometimes forget their dreams. In the nature of the case such a theory is hard to refute, but perhaps the burden of proof should be put on the propounders of the theory.

Why do we have the same dream repeatedly? This is a curious fact for which no definite explanation can be given. However, in such repeated dreams we are able to find the style of life expressed with much more clarity. Such a repeated dream gives us a definite and unmistakable indication where the individual goal of superiority lies.

In the case of long and extended dreams we must believe that the dreamer is not fully ready. He is looking for the bridge from the problem to the attainment of the goal. For this reason the dreams which can be best understood are short dreams. Sometimes a dream consists of only one picture, a few words, and it shows how the dreamer is really trying to find a short way to deceive himself.

We may close our discussion with the question of sleep. A great many persons put to themselves needless questions about sleep. They imagine that sleep is the contradiction of being awake, and that it is the "brother of death," But such views are erroneous. Sleep is not a contradiction of being awake, but is rather a degree of being awake. We are not separated from life in sleep. On the contrary we are thinking, and hearing in sleep. The same tendencies are generally expressed in sleep as in waking life. Thus there are mothers who cannot be awakened by any of the street noises, but if the children move in the least bit they immediately jump up. We see how their interest is really awake. Also from the fact that we do not fall out of bed we can see that we realize limits in sleep.

The whole personality is expressed by night and by day. This explains the phenomena of hypnotism. What superstition has made to appear as a magic power is for the most nothing more than a variety of sleep. But it is a variety in which one person wants to obey another and knows that the second person wants to make him sleep. A simple form of the same thing is when parents say, "It is enough now sleep!" and the children obey. In hypnotism, too, the results take place because the person is obedient. And in proportion to his obedience is the ease with which he may become hynotized.

In hypnotism we have an opportunity of making a person create pictures, ideas, remembrances which he would not do with his waking inhibitions. The only requirement is obedience. By this method we can find some solutions some old remembrances which may have been forgotten before.

As a method of treatment and cure, hypnotism has its dangers, however. The present writer does not like hypnotism and uses it only when a patient trusts no other method. One will find that hypnotized persons are rather revengeful. In the beginning they overcome their difficulties, but they do not really change their style of life. It is like a drug or a mechanical means: the person's true nature has not been touched. What we have to do is to give a person courage, selfconfidence and better understanding of his mistakes, if we are really to help him. Hypnotism does not do this, and should not be used except in rare cases.

CHAPTER EIGHT

PROBLEM CHILDREN
AND THEIR EDUCATION

HOW shall we educate our children? This is perhaps the most important question in our present social life. It is a question to which Individual Psychology has a great deal to contribute. Education, whether carried on in the home or at school, is an attempt to bring out and direct the personalities of individuals. Psychological science is thus a necessary basis for the proper educational technique, or if we will, we may look upon all education as a branch of that vast psychological art of living.

Let us begin with certain preliminaries. The most general principle of education is that it must be consistent with the later life which the individuals will be called upon to face. This means that it must be consistent with the ideals of the nation. If we do not educate children with the ideals of the nation in view, then these children are likely to encounter difficulties later in life. They will not fit in as members of society.

To be sure the ideals of a nation may change they may change suddenly, as after a revolution, or gradually, in the process of evolution. But this simply means that the educator should keep in mind a very broad ideal. It should be an ideal which will always have its place, and which will teach the individual to adjust himself properly to changing circumstances.

The connection of schools with social ideals is of course due to their connection with the government. It is the influence of the government which causes national ideals to be reflected in the school system. The government does not readily reach the parents or the family, but it watches the schools in its own behalf.

Historically, the schools have reflected different ideals at different periods. In Europe schools were originally established for aristocratic families. The schools were aristocratic in spirit, and only aristocrats were taught in them. Later on, the schools were taken over by the churches, and they appeared as religious schools. Only priests were teachers. Then the demands of the nation for more knowledge began to increase. More subjects were sought and a greater number of teachers was needed than the church could supply. In this way others besides priests and clergymen entered the profession.

Until quite modern times the teachers were never exclusively teachers. They followed many other trades, such as shoemaking, tailoring, etc. It is obvious that they knew how to teach only by using the rod. Their schools were not the sort in which the psychological problems of the children could be solved.

The beginning of the modern spirit in education was made in Europe in Pestalozzi's time. Pestalozzi was the first teacher to find other teaching methods besides the rod and punishment.

Pestalozzi is valuable for us because he showed the great importance of methods in the schools. With correct methods, every child unless he is feeble-minded can learn to read, to write, to sing, and to do arithmetic. We cannot say that we have already discovered the best methods; they are in the process of development all the time. As is right and proper, we are always searching for new and better methods.

To return to the history of European schools, it is to be noted that just after pedagogical technique had developed to some extent, there appeared a great need for workmen who could read, write, count, and be generally independent without needing constant guidance. At this time there appeared the slogan, "a school for every child." At present every child is forced to go to school. This development is due to the conditions of our economic life and to the ideals which reflect these conditions.

Formerly in Europe only aristocrats were influential, and there was

89

a demand only for officials and for laborers. Those who had to be prepared for higher stations went to higher schools; the rest did not go to school at all. The educational system reflected the national ideals of the time. Today the school system corresponds to a different set of national ideals. We no longer have schools in which children must sit quietly, hands folded in their laps, and not allowed to move. We now have schools in which the children are the teacher's friends. They are no longer compelled by authority, no longer compelled merely to obey, but are allowed to develop more independently. Naturally there are many such schools in democratic United States, since the schools always develop with the ideals of a country as crystallized in governmental regulations.

The connection of the school system with national and social ideals is organic due to their origin and organization, as we have seen but from a psychological point of view it gives them a great advantage as an educational agency. From a psychological point of view the principal aim of education is social adjustment. Now the school can guide the current of sociability in the individual child more easily than the family because it is much nearer to the demands of the nation and more independent of the criticism of the children. It does not pamper the children, and in general it has a much more detached attitude.

On the other hand the family is not always permeated with the social ideal. Too often we find traditional ideas dominating there. Only when the parents are themselves socially adjusted and understand that the aim of education must be social, can progress be made. Wherever parents know and understand these things we will find children rightly educated and prepared for school, just as in school they are rightly prepared for their special place in life. This should be the ideal development of the child at home and in school, with the school standing midway between the family and the nation.

We have gathered from previous discussions that the style of life of a child in a family is fixed after it is four or five years old and cannot directly be changed. This indicates the way in which the modern school has to go. It must not criticise or punish, but try to mould, educate and develop the social interest of children. The modern school cannot work on the principle of suppression and censorship, but rather on the idea of trying to understand and solve the personal problems of the child.

On the other hand, parents and children being so closely united in the family, it is often difficult for the former to educate the latter for society. They prefer to educate the children for their own sakes, and thereby they create a tendency which will conflict with the situation of the child in later life. Such children are bound to face great difficulties. They are already confronted with them the moment they enter school, and the problems become still more difficult in life after school.

To remedy this situation it is of course necessary to educate the parents. Often this is not easy, for we cannot always lay our hands on the elders as we do on the children. And even when we get to the parents, we may find that they are not very much interested in the ideals of the nation. They are so set in tradition that they do not want to understand.

Not being able to do much with the parents, we simply have to content ourselves with spreading more understanding everywhere. The best point of attack is our schools. This is true first because the large numbers of children are gathered there; secondly, because mistakes in the style of life appear better there than in the family; and, thirdly, because the teacher is supposedly a person who understands the problems of children.

Normal children, if there be such, do not concern us. We would not touch them. If we see children who are fully developed and socially adjusted, the best thing is not to suppress them. They should go their own way, because such children can be depended upon to look for a goal on the useful side in order to develop the sense of superiority. Their superiority feeling, precisely because it is on the useful side, is not a superiority complex.

91

On the other hand both the feeling of superiority and the feeling of inferiority exist on the useless side among problem children, neurotics, criminals, etc. Such persons express a superiority complex as a compensation for their inferiority complex. The feeling of inferiority, as we have shown, exists in every human being, but this feeling becomes a complex only when it discourages him to the point of stimulating training on the useless side of life.

All these problems of inferiority and superiority have their root in family life during the period before the child enters school. It is during this period that he has built up his style of life, which in contrast with the adult style of life we have designated as a prototype. This prototype is the unripe fruit, and like an unripe fruit, if there is some trouble with it, if there is a worm, the more it develops and ripens the larger the worm grows.

As we have seen, the worm or difficulty develops from problems over imperfect organs. It is the difficulty with imperfect organs that is the usual root of the feeling of inferiority, and here again we must remember that it is not the organic inferiority that causes the problem but the social maladjustments which it brings in its wake. It is this that provides the educational opportunity. Train a person to adjust himself socially and the organic inferiorities, so far from being liabilities, may become assets. For as we have seen, an organic inferiority may be the origin of a very striking interest, developed through training, which may rule the individual's whole life, and provided this interest runs in a useful channel, it may mean a great deal to the individual.

It all depends on the way the organic difficulty fits in with the social adjustment. Thus in the case of a child who wants only to see, or only to hear, it is up to the teacher to develop his interest in the use of all his sense organs. Otherwise he will be out of line with the rest of the pupils.

We are all familiar with the case of the left-handed child who grows up clumsy. As a rule no one realizes that this child is left-handed and that this accounts for his clumsiness. Because of his left-handedness he is constantly at odds with the family. We find that such children either become fighting or aggressive children which is an advantage or else they become depressed and peevish. When such a child goes to school with his problems, we shall find him either combative, or else downhearted, irritable and lacking in courage.

Besides the children with imperfect organs, a problem is presented by the great number of pampered children who come to school. Now the way schools are organized, it is physically impossible for a single child always to remain the center of attention. It may indeed happen occasionally that a teacher is so kind and soft-hearted that she plays favorites, but as the child moves from grade to grade it falls out of its position of favor. Later in life it is even worse, for it is not considered proper in our civilization for one person always to be the center of attention, without doing anything to merit it.

All such problem children have certain defined characteristics. They are not well fitted for the problems of life; they are very ambitious, and want to rule personally, not in behalf of society. In addition they are always quarrelsome and at enmity with others. They are usually cowards, since they lack interest in all the problems of life. A pampered childhood has not prepared them for life's problems.

Other characteristics which we discover among such children is that they are cautious and continually hesitating. They postpone the solution of the problems that life presents to them. Or else they come to a stop altogether before problems, going off on distractions and never finishing anything.

These characteristics come to light more clearly in school than in the family. School is like an experiment or acid test, for there it becomes apparent whether or not a child is adjusted to society and its problems. A mistaken style of life often escapes unrecognized at home, but it comes out in school.

Both the pampered-child and the organ-inferiority type of children always want to "exclude" the difficulties of life because of their

93

great feeling of inferiority which robs them of strength to cope with them. However, we may control the difficulties at school, and thus gradually put them in a position to solve problems. The school thus becomes a place where we really educate, and not merely give instruction.

Besides these two types, we have to consider the hated child. The hated child is usually ugly, mistaken, crippled, and in no way prepared for social life. He has, perhaps, the greatest difficulty of all three types upon entering school.

We see, then, that whether or not teachers and officials like it, an understanding of all these problems and of the best methods for handling them must be developed as part of the school adminstration.

Besides these specifically problem children, there are also the children who are believed to be prodigies the exceptionally bright children. Sometimes because they are ahead in some subjects it is easy for them to appear brilliant in others. They are sensitive, ambitious, and not usually very well liked by their comrades. Children immediately seem to feel whether one of their number is socially adjusted or not. Such prodigies are admired but not beloved.

We can understand how many of these prodigies pass through school satisfactorily. But when they enter social life they have no adequate plan of life. When they approach the three great problems of life society, occupation, and love and marriage their difficulties come out. What happened in their prototype years becomes apparent, and we see the effect of their not being well adjusted in the family. There they continually found themselves in favorable situations, which did not bring out the mistakes in their style of life. But the moment that a new situation comes their way, the mistakes appear.

It is interesting to note that poets have seen the connection between these things. A great many poets and dramatists have described, in

94

their dramas and romances, the very complicated current of life seen in such persons. There is for example, Shakespeare's character, Northumberland. Shakespeare, who was a master of psychology, portrays Northumberland as quite loyal to his king until real danger came. Then he betrayed him. Shakespeare understood the fact that the true style of life of a person becomes apparent under very difficult circumstances. But it is not the difficult circumstances that produce the style it has been built up before.

The solution that Individual Psychology offers for the problems of prodigies is the same as that for other problem children. The individual psychologist says, "Everybody can accomplish everything." This is a democratic maxim which takes the edge off prodigies, who are always burdened with expectations, are always pushed forward and become too much interested in their own persons. Persons who adopt this maxim can have very brilliant children, and these children do not have to become conceited or too ambitious. They understand that what they have accomplished was the result of training and good fortune. If their good training is continued they can accomplish whatever others can accomplish. But other children, who are less favorably influenced and not as well trained and educated, may also accomplish good things if their teacher can make them understand the method.

These latter children may have lost courage. They must therefore be protected against their marked feeling of inferiority, a feeling that none of us can suffer for long. Originally such children were not confronted with as many difficulties as they now meet at school. One can understand their being overwhelmed by these difficulties and wanting to play truant or else not go to school at all. They believe that there is no hope for them at school, and if this belief were true we should have to agree that they are acting consistently and rationally. But Individual Psychology does not accept the belief that their case is hopeless at school. It believes that everybody can accomplish useful works. There are always mistakes, but these can be corrected and the child can go on.

In the usual circumstances, however, the situation is not handled

95

properly. At the very time when the child is overwhelmed by the new difficulties at school, the mother takes on a watching and anxious attitude. The school reports, the criticisms and scoldings that the child gets at school are magnified by the repercussions at home. Very often a child who has been a good child at home, because he has been pampered, becomes very bad in school because his latent inferiority complex shows up the moment he loses contact with the family. It is then that the pampering mother will be hated by such a child because he feels that she has deceived him. She does not appear in the same light as she did before. All her old behavior and pampering is forgotten in the anxiety of the new situation.

We find very often that a child, who is a fighting child at home, is quiet, calm, and even suppressed at school. Sometimes the mother comes to school and says, "This child occupies me the entire day. He is always fighting." The teacher says, "He sits quietly all day and does not move." And sometimes we have the reverse. That is, the mother comes and says, "This child is very quiet and sweet at home," while the teacher says, "He corrupts my whole class." We can easily understand the last situation. The child is the center of attention at home and for that reason is quiet and unassuming. In school he is not the center of attention, and so he fights. Or it may be the other way around.

There is the case, for example, of a girl eight years old, who was very well liked by her schoolmates and was head of her class. Her father came to the doctor saying, "This child is very sadistic a veritable tyrant. We can no longer bear her." What was the reason? She was a first child in a weak family. Only a weak family could be so tortured by a child. When another child was born this girl felt herself in danger, and still wanting to be the center of attention as before, she began to fight. At school she was quite appreciated, and not having any reason to fight she developed well.

Some children have difficulty both at home and in school. Both family and school complain, and the result is that the children's mistakes increase. Some are untidy at home and in school. Now if the behavior is the same both within the family and at school, we must look for the cause in things that have gone before. In any case we must always consider both the actions in the family and in school in order to form a judgment on a child's problems. Every part becomes important for us if we are correctly to understand his style of life and the direction in which he is striving.

It -sometimes happens that a fairly well-adjusted child, when he encounters the new situations in school, may not seem adjusted. This usually happens when a child comes to a school where the teacher and the pupils are very much against him. To take an example from European experience, a child not an aristocrat, comes to an aristocratic school, being sent there because his parents are very rich and conceited. Since he is not of an aristocratic family, his comrades are all against him. Here is a child, previously pampered or at least comfortably adjusted, who suddenly finds himself in a very hostile atmosphere. Sometimes the cruelty of such comrades can reach such a point that it is really astonishing for a child to be able to stand it. In most cases the child never speaks a word about it at home because he feels ashamed. He suffers his terrible ordeal in silence.

Often such children when they come to the age of sixteen or eighteen years the age when they have to behave towards society like adults and face life's problems squarely stop short because they have lost courage and hope. And along with their social handicaps goes their handicap in love and marriage because they cannot go on.

What are we to do with such cases? They have no outlet for their energies. They are separated, or feel separated from the whole world. The type of person who wants to hurt himself for the sake of hurting others may commit suicide. On the other hand there is the type who wants to disappear. He disappears in an asylum. He loses even the few social abilities he had before. He does not speak in the common way, does not approach people, and is always antagonistic towards the whole world. This state we call dementia praecox, insanity. If we are to help any of these we must find a way to rebuild their courage. They are very difficult cases, but they can be cured.

Inasmuch as the treatment and cure of children's educational problems depend primarily upon the diagnosis of their style of life, it is well to review here the methods that Individual Psychology has developed for this diagnosis. The diagnosis of the style of life is of course useful for many other things besides education, but it is quite essential in educational practice.

Besides direct study of a child during his formative years, Individual Psychology uses the methods of asking for old remembrances and fancies concerning future occupations, the observation of posture and bodily movements, and certain inferences from the order of the child in the family. We have discussed all these methods before, but it is perhaps necessary to emphasize again the position of the child in the family, as this is more closely connected with educational development than the other methods.

The important thing about the order of children in the family is, as we have seen, that a first child is for a while in a position of an only child and is later dethroned from that position. He thus enjoys great power for a while, only to lose it. On the other hand the psychology of the other children is fixed and determined by the fact that they are not first children.

Among oldest children we often find a conservative view prevailing. They have the feeling that those in power should remain in power. It is only an accident that they have lost their power and they have great admiration for it.

The second child is in an entirely different situation. He goes along, not as the center of attention, but with a pace-maker running before him. He always wants to equal him. He does not recognize power, but wants power to change hands. He feels a forward urge as in a race. All his movements show that he is looking at a point ahead in order to catch up to it. He is always trying to change the laws of

98

science and nature. He is really revolutionary not so much in politics, but in social life and in his attitude toward his fellows. We have a good example in the biblical story of Jacob and Esau.

In a case where there are several children who are nearly grown up before another is born, the latest child finds himself in a situation similar to that of a first child.

The position of the youngest in the family is of remarkable interest from a psychological viewpoint. By youngest we mean of course the child that is always the youngest and never has any successors. Such a child is in an advantageous position since he can never be dethroned. The second child may be dethroned, and sometimes he experiences the tragedy of the first child, but this can never happen in the life of the youngest child. He is therefore the most favorably situated, and other circumstances being equal, we find that the youngest child gets the best development. He resembles the second child in that he is very energetic and tries to overcome others. He, too, has pace-makers to outdistance. But in general he takes an entirely different way from the rest of the family. If the family be one of scientists, the youngest will probably be a musician or a merchant. If the family be one of merchants, the youngest may be a poet. He must always be different. For it is easier not to have to compete in the same field but to work in another one, and for that reason he likes to follow a different line from the rest. Obviously, this is a sign that he is somewhat lacking in courage, for were such a child courageous, he would compete in the same field.

It is worthy of note that our predictions based on the position of children are expressed in the form of tendencies; there is no necessity about them. And in fact if a first child is bright, he may not at all be conquered by the second, and thus will not suffer any tragedy. Such a child is socially well-adjusted, and his mother is likely to have spread his interest toward others, including the newborn baby. On the other hand if this first child cannot really be conquered, then it is a greater difficulty for the second, and this second child may become a problem. Such second children result in the worst types, because they often lose courage, and hope. We know that children in a race must always have the hope of winning; and when this hope is gone, all is lost.

The only child also has his tragedy, for he has been the center of attention in the family throughout his childhood, and his goal in life is always to be the center. He does not reason along the lines of logic, but along the lines of his own style of life.

The position of an only boy among a family of girls is also difficult and presents a problem. It is commonly supposed that such a boy behaves in a girlish manner, but this view is rather exaggerated. After all, we are all educated by women. However, there is a certain amount of difficulty, inasmuch as the whole family in such a case is established for women. One can immediately tell upon entering a house, whether the family has more boys or girls. The furniture is different, there is more or less noise, and the order is different. There are more broken things where there are more boys, and everything is much cleaner where there are more girls in the family.

A boy in such an environment may strive to appear more of a man and exaggerate this feature of his character; or else he may indeed grow girlish like the rest of the household. In short we will find that such a boy is either soft and mild or else very wild. In the latter eventually it would seem that he is always trying to prove and emphasize the fact that he is a man.

The only girl among boys is in an equally difficult situation. Either she is very quiet and develops very femminely, or else she wants to do everything that the boys do and to develop like them. A feeling of inferiority is quite apparent in such a case, since she is the only girl in a situation where boys are superior. The inferiority complex lies in the feeling that she is only a girl. In this word "only" the whole inferiority complex is expressed. We see the development of a compensating superiority complex when she tries to dress like the boys and when later in life she wants to have the sexual relations that she understands men have.

We may conclude our discussion of the position of a child in a

100

family with the peculiar case where the first child is a boy and the second a girl. Here there is always a fierce competition between the two. The girl is pushed forward not only because she is the second child but also because she is a girl. She trains more, and thus becomes a very marked type of second child. She is very energetic and very independent, and the boy notices how she always approaches nearer and nearer to him in the race. As we know it is a fact that girls develop more rapidly physically and mentally than boys a girl of twelve, for instance, is much more developed than a boy of the same age. The boy sees this and cannot explain it. Hence he feels inferior and has a longing to give up. He does not progress any more. Instead he starts looking for escapes. Sometimes he develops ways of escape in the direction of art. At other times he becomes neurotic, criminal, or insane. He does not feel strong enough to go on with the race.

This type of situation is a difficult one to solve even with the viewpoint that "Everybody can accomplish everything." The main thing we can do is to show the boy that if the girl seems to be ahead it is only because she practices more and by practicing finds better methods for development. We can also seek to direct the girl and the boy into non-competitive fields, as far as possible, so as to diminish the atmosphere of running a race.

CHAPTER NINE

SOCIAL PROBLEMS
AND SOCIAL ADJUSTMENT

The goal of Individual Psychology is H social adjustment. This may seem a paradox, but if it is a paradox, it is so only verbally. The fact is that it is only when we pay attention to the concrete psychological life of the individual do we come to realize how all-important is the social element. The individual becomes an individual only in a social context. Other systems of psychology make a distinction between what they call individual psychology and social psychology, but for us there is no such distinction. Our discussions hitherto have attempted to analyze the individual style of life, but the analysis has always been with a social point of view and for a social application.

We now continue our analysis with more emphasis on the problems of social adjustment. The realities to be discussed are the same, but instead of concentrating our attention on diagnosing styles of life, we shall discuss the styles of life in action and the methods for furthering proper action.

The analysis of social problems continues directly on our analysis of the problems of educational upbringing, which was the theme of our last chapter. The school and nursery are miniature social institutions, and we can study there the problems of social maladjustment in a simplified form.

Take the behavior problems of a boy of five. A mother came to the doctor complaining that her boy was restless, hyperactive, and very troublesome. She was always occupied with him and at the end of the day was exhausted. She said she could not stand the boy any more and was willing to have him removed from the house if such a treatment was advisable.

From these behavior details we can readily "identify" with the boy we can readily put ourselves in his place. If we hear that a child of five is hyperactive, we can easily imagine what his line of conduct would be. What would anyone do if he were that age and hyperactive? He would climb on the table with his heavy shoes. He would always like to go about dirty. And if the mother wanted to read, he would play with the lights and turn them on and off. Or again if the mother and father wanted to play the piano or wanted to sing together what would such a boy do! He would yell. Or else hold his ears and insist that he did not like such a noise. He would always have temper tantrums if he did not get what he wanted and he would always want something.

If we note such behavior in the nursery school, we may be sure that such a boy wants to fight and that everything he does is done in order to induce a fight. He is restless day and night, while his father and mother are always tired. The boy is never tired because unlike his parents he does not have to do what he does not want. He simply wants to be restless and occupy the others.

A particular incident well illustrates how this boy fought for the center of attention. One day he was taken to a concert at which his mother and father played and sang. In the middle of a song the boy called out, "Hello daddy!" and walked all around the hall. One could have predieted this, but the mother and father did not understand the reason for such behavior. They regarded him as a normal child, in spite of the fact that he did not behave normally.

To this extent he was, however, normal: he had an intelligent plan of life. What he did was rightly done, in accordance with his plan. And if we see the plan we can guess the actions that result. Hence we may conclude that he is not feeble-minded, for a feeble-minded person never has an intelligent plan of life.

When his mother had visitors and wanted to enjoy the party, he would push the visitors off the chairs and always wanted the particular chair upon which one was about to sit. We see how this, too, is consistent with his goal and with his prototype. His goal is to be superior and to rule others, and always to occupy the attention of his father and mother.

We can judge that he used to be a pampered child, and that were he to be pampered again he would not fight. In other words, it is a child who has lost his favorable situation.

How did he lose his favorable situation? The answer is, he must have acquired a younger brother or sister. He is thus a five-year-old in a new situation, feeling dethroned and fighting to* hold his important central position which he believes to have lost. For that reason he keeps his father and mother always occupied with him. Also there is another reason. One can see that the boy has not been prepared for the new situation and that in his position of pampered child he never developed any communal feeling. He is thus not socially adjusted. He is interested only in himself and occupied only with his own welfare.

When his mother was asked how the boy behaved towards the younger brother, she insisted that he liked him, but that whenever he played with him he always knocked him down. We might be pardoned for presuming that such actions do not indicate marked affection.

To understand fully the significance of this behavior we should compare it to the cases we frequently meet of fighting children who do not fight continuously. The children are too intelligent to fight continuously, for they know that the father and mother would put an end to their fighting. Hence such children from time to time stop their fighting and go on their good behavior. But the old movement reappears, as it does in this case when, in the course of his playing with the younger brother, he knocks him down. His goal in playing is in fact to knock him down.

Now what is the boy's behavior towards his mother? If she tries to spank him, he either laughs and insists that the spanking does not hurt him; or else, if she beats him a little harder, he becomes quiet for a while, only to begin his fighting a little later. One should

104

notice how all the boy's behavior is conditioned by his goal and how everything he does is rightly directed towards it so much so that we can predict his actions. We could not predict them if the prototype were not a unity, or if we did not know the goal of the prototype's movement.

Imagine this boy starting out in life. He goes to the nursery school, and we can predict what will happen there. We could have predicted what would happen if the boy were to be taken to a concert, as he actually was. In general he will rule in a weak environment, or, in a more difficult one, he will fight to rule. And so his stay at the nursery school is likely to be shortened if the teacher is severe. In that case the boy might try to find subterfuges. He would be in a constant tension, and this tension might make him suffer from headache, restlessness, etc. The symptoms would appear as the first indications of a neurosis.

On the other hand if the environment were soft and pleasant, he might feel that he was the center of attention. Under such circumstances he might even become the leader of the school the complete champion.

The nursery school, as we can see, is a social institution with social problems. An individual must be prepared for such problems because he has to follow the laws of the community. The child must be able to make himself useful to that little community, and he cannot be useful unless he is more interested in others than in himself.

In public school the same situation is repeated, and we can imagine what would happen to a boy of this sort. Things might be a little easier in a private school, since in such a school there are generally fewer pupils, to whom more attention can be paid. Perhaps in such an environment no one could notice that he was a problem child. Perhaps they might even say instead, "This is our most brilliant boy, our best pupil." It is also possible that if he were the head of the class, his behavior at home might change. He might be satisfied to be superior in one way only.

105

In cases where a child's behavior improves after he goes to school, one may take it for granted that he has a favorable situation in his class and feels superior there. Usually, however, the contrary is true. Children who are very much loved and very obedient at home often corrupt the class at school.

We have spoken in the last chapter of the school as standing midway between the home and life in society. If we apply that formula we can understand what happens to a boy of our type when he goes out into life. Life will not offer him the favorable situation which he may sometimes find in school. People are often surprised and cannot understand how children who are brilliant at home and brilliant in school should turn out in later life worthless. We have here problem adults with a neurosis which may later turn into insanity. No one understands such cases because the prototype has been covered over by favorable situations until the age of adult life.

On this account we must learn to understand the mistaken prototype in the favorable situation, or at least to realize that it may exist, since it is very difficult to recognize it there. There are a few signs which may be taken as definite indications of a mistaken prototype. A child who wants to attract attention and who is lacking in social interest will often be untidy. By being untidy he occupies other people's time. He will also not want to go to sleep, and will cry out at night or wet the bed. He plays at anxiety because he has noticed that anxiety is a weapon by which he may force others to obey. All these signs appear in favorable situations, and by looking for them one is likely to reach a correct conclusion.

Let us look at this boy with the mistaken prototype later in life, when he is on the verge of maturity say at 17 or 18. There is a great hinterland of life behind him a hinterland which is not so easily evaluated because it is not very distinct. It is not easy to see the goal and the style of life. But as he faces life he has to meet what we have called the three great questions of life the social question, the question of occupation, and that of love and marriage. These questions arise out of the relationships bound up in our very

106

existence. The social question involves our behavior towards other people, our attitude to mankind and the future of mankind. This question involves the preservation and the salvation of man. For human life is so limited that we can carry on only if we pull together.

As regards occupation, we can judge from what we have seen of the boy's behavior at school. We can be sure that if the boy seeks an occupation with the idea of being superior, he will have difficulty in obtaining such a position. It is difficult to find a position where one will not be subordinate, or where one will not have to work with others. But as this boy is interested only in his own welfare, he will never get along well in a subordinate position. Moreover, such a person does not prove very trustworthy in business. He can never subordinate his own interest to the interest of the firm.

In general we may say that success in an occupation is dependent on social adjustment. It is a great advantage in business to be able to understand the needs of neighbors and customers, to see with their eyes, hear with their ears, and feel as they feel. Such persons will move ahead, but this boy that we are studying cannot do so, for he is always looking out for his own interests. He can develop only a part of what is necessary for progress. Hence he will often be a failure in his occupation.

In most cases one will find that such persons never finish their preparation for an occupation, or at least, are late in taking up an occupation. They are perhaps thirty years old, and do not know what they intend to do in life. They frequently change from one course of study to another, or from one type of position to another. This is a sign that they cannot be suited in any way.

Sometimes we find a youth of 17 or 18 who is striving, but does not know what to do. It is important to be able to understand such a person and to advise him regarding the choice of a vocation. He can still get interested in something from the beginning and train properly.

107

On the other hand it is rather disturbing to find a boy of this age not knowing what he wants to do in later life. He is too often the type that does not accomplish much. Both at home and at school efforts ought to be made to interest boys' thoughts in their future occupations before they reach this age. In school this might be done by giving composition assignments on such topics as "What I want to be later in life." If they are asked to write on such a theme, they are definitely confronted with the question, which otherwise they might never face until it is too late.

The last question that our youth has to face is that of love and marriage. Inasmuch as we are living as two separate sexes, this is an all-important question. It would be very different if we were all one sex. As it is, we have to train in ways of behaving towards the other sex. We shall discuss the question of love and marriage at length in a succeeding chapter: here it is only necessary to show its connection with the problems of social adjustment. The same lack of social interest which is responsible for social and occupational maladjustments is also responsible for the common inabilities to meet the other sex properly. A person who is exclusively selfcentered has not the proper preparation for a manage a deux. Indeed it would seem that one of the chief purposes of the sex instinct is to pull the individual out of his narrow shell and to prepare him for social life. But psychologically we have to meet the sex instinct half-way it cannot accomplish its function properly unless we are already predisposed to forget our own self and merge it in a larger life.

We may now draw some conclusions about this boy we have been studying. We have seen him stand before the three great questions of life, despairing and afraid of defeat. We have seen him with his personal goal of superiority excluding as far as possible all the questions of life. What then is left for him? He will not join in society, he is antagonistic to others, he is very suspicious and seclusive. And being no longer interested in others, he does not care how he appears before them, and so he will often be ragged and dirty with all the appearance of an insane person. Language we know is a social necessity, but our subject does not wish to use it. He does not speak at all a trait that is to be seen in dementia praecox.

Blocked by a self-imposed blockade from all the questions of life, the way of our subject leads straight to the asylum. His goal of superiority brings about a hermetical isolation from others, and it transforms his sex drives so that he is no longer a normal person. We find him sometimes trying to fly to heaven, or thinking himself to be Jesus Christ or the Emperor of China. In this way he manages to express his goal of superiority.

As we have frequently said, all the problems of life are at bottom social problems. We see social problems expressed in the nursery school, the public school, in friendship, in politics, in economic life, etc. It is evident that all our abilities are socially focussed and directed for the use of mankind.

We know that a lack in social adjustment begins in the prototype. The question is how to correct this lack before it is too late. If the parents could be told not only how to prevent the great mistakes but also how to diagnose the little expressions of the mistakes in the prototype and how to correct them, it would be a great advantage. But the truth is it is not possible to accomplish much in this way. Few parents are inclined to learn and to avoid mistakes. They are not interested in questions of psychology and education. Either they pamper the children and are antagonistic to anyone who does not regard their children as perfect jewels, or else they are not interested at all. Not much can thus be accomplished through them. Also it is impossible to give them a good understanding in a short time. It would take a great deal of time to tell parents and advise them of what they should know. It is much better, therefore, to call in a physician or psychologist.

Outside of the individual work of the physician and psychologist, the best results can be accomplished only through schools and education. Mistakes in the prototype often do not appear until a child enters school. A teacher cognizant of the methods of

Individual Psychology will notice a mistaken prototype in a short time. She can see whether a child joins the others, or wants to be the center of attention by pushing himself forward. She also sees which children have courage and which lack it. A well-taught teacher could understand the mistakes of a prototype in the first week.

Teachers, by the very nature of their social function, are better equipped, to correct the mistakes of children. Mankind started schools because the family was not able to educate children adequately for the social demands of life. The school is the prolonged hand of the family, and it is there that the character of a child is formed to a great extent, and that he is taught to face the problems of life.

All that is necessary is that the schools and teachers should be equipped with psychological insight which will enable them to perform their task properly. In the future schools will surely be run more along the lines of Individual Psychology, for the true purpose of a school is to build character.

CHAPTER TEN

SOCIAL FEELING, COMMON SENSE AND THE INFERIORITY COMPLEX

WE have seen that social maladjustments are caused by the social consequences of the sense of inferiority and the striving for superiority. The terms inferiority complex and superiority complex already express the result after a maladjustment has taken place. These complexes are not in the germplasm, they are not in the blood-stream: they simply happen in the course of the interaction of the individual and his social environment. Why don't they happen to all individuals? All individuals have a sense of inferiority and a striving for success and superiority which makes up the very life of the psyche. The reason all individuals do not have complexes is that their sense of inferiority and superiority is harnessed by a psychological mechanism into socially useful channels. The springs of this mechanism are social interest, courage, and social-mindedness, or the logic of common sense.

Let us study both the functioning and nonfunctioning of this mechanism. As long as the feeling of inferiority is not too great, we know that a child will always strive to be worth while and on the useful side of life. Such a child, in order to gain his end, is interested in others. Social feeling and social adjustment are the right and normal compensations, and in a sense it is almost impossible to find anybody child or adult in whom the striving for superiority has not resulted in such development. We can never find anyone who could say truly, "I am not interested in others." He may act this way he may act as if he were not interested in the world but he cannot justify himself. Rather does he claim to be interested in others, in order to hide his lack of social adjustment. This is mute testimony to the universality of the social feeling.

Nonetheless maladjustments do take place. We can study their genesis by considering marginal cases cases where an inferiority

111

complex exists but is not openly expressed on account of a favorable environment. The complex is then hidden, or at least a tendency to hide it is shown. Thus if a person is not confronted with a difficulty, he may look wholly satisfied. But if we look closely we shall see how he really expresses if not in words or opinions, at least in attitudes the fact that he feels inferior. This is an inferiority complex and is the result of an exaggerated feeling of inferiority. People who are suffering from such a complex are always looking for relief from the burdens which they have imposed upon themselves through their self-centeredness. It is rather interesting to observe how some persons hide their inferiority complex, while others confess, "I am suffering from an inferiority complex." The confessors are always elated at their confession. They feel greater than others because they have confessed while others cannot. They say to themselves, "I am honest. I do not lie about the cause of my suffering." But at the very moment that they confess their inferiority complex, they hint at some difficulties in their lives or other circumstances which are responsible for their situation. They may speak of their parents or family, of not being well educated, or of some accident, curtailment, suppression, or other things.

Often the inferiority complex may be hidden by a superiority complex, which serves as a compensation. Such persons are arrogant, impertinent, conceited and snobbish. They lay more weight on appearances than on actions.

In the early strivings of a man of this type one may find a certain stage fright, which is thereafter used to excuse all the person's failures. He says, "If I did not suffer from stage fright, what could I not do!" These sentences with "if" generally hide an inferiority complex.

An inferiority complex may also be indicated by such characteristics as slyness, cautiousness, pedantry, the exclusion of the greater problems of life, and the search for a narrow field of action which is limited by many principles and rules. It is also a sign of an inferiority complex if a person always leans on a stick.

112

Such a person does not trust himself, and we will find that he develops queer interests. He is always occupied with little things, such as collecting newspapers or advertisements. They waste their time this way and always excuse themselves. They train too much on the useless side, and this training when long continued leads to a compulsion neurosis.

An inferiority complex is usually hidden in all problem children no matter what type of problem the children present on the surface. Thus to be lazy is in reality to exclude the important tasks of life and is a sign of a complex. To steal is to take advantage of the insecurity or absence of another; to lie is not to have the courage to tell the truth. All these manifestations in children have an inferiority complex as their core.

A neurosis is a developed form of inferiority complex. What can a person not accomplish when he is suffering from an anxiety neurosis! He may be constantly striving to have someone accompany him; if so, he succeeds in his purpose. He is supported by others and gets others to be occupied with him. Here we see the transition from an inferiority to a superiority complex. Other people must serve! In getting other people to serve, the neurotic becomes superior. A similar evolution is manifested in the case of insane persons. After having been forced into difficulties because of the policy of exclusion engendered by an inferiority complex, they become successful in an imaginary way by regarding themselves as great persons.

In all these cases where complexes develop, the failure to function in social and useful channels is due to a lack of courage on the part of the individual. It is this lack of courage which prevents him from following the social course. Side by side with the lack of courage are the intellectual accompaniments of a failure to understand the necessity and utility of the social course.

All this is most clearly illustrated in the behavior of criminals who are really cases of inferiority complexes par excellence. Criminals

113

are cowardly and stupid; their cowardice and social stupidity go together as two parts of the same tendency.

Drinking may be analyzed on similar lines. The drunkard seeks relief from his problems, and is cowardly enough to be satisfied with the relief that comes from the useless side of life.

The ideology and intellectual outlook of such persons differentiate themselves sharply from the social common sense which accompanies the courageous attitudes of normal persons. Criminals, for instance, always make excuses or accuse others. They mention unprofitable conditions of labor. They speak of the cruelty of society in not supporting them. Or they say the stomach commands and cannot be ruled. When sentenced, they always find such excuses as that of the child-murderer Hickman, who said, "It was done by a command from above." Another murderer, upon being sentenced, said, "What is the use of such a boy as I have killed? There are a million other boys." Then there is the "philosopher," who claims that it is not bad to kill an old woman with a lot of money, when so many worth-while people are starving.

The logic of such arguments strikes us as quite frail, and it is frail. The whole outlook is conditioned by their socially useless goal, just as the selection of that goal is conditioned by their lack of courage. They always have to justify themselves, whereas a goal on the useful side of life goes without saying and does not need any excuses in its favor.

Let us take some actual clinical cases which illustrate how social attitudes and goals are transformed into anti-social ones. Our first case is of a girl who was nearly fourteen. She grew up in an honest family. The father, a hardworking man, had supported the family as long as he was able to work, but he had taken sick. The mother was a good and honest woman and was very much interested in her children, who were six in all. The first child was a brilliant girl, who died at the age of twelve. The second girl was sick, but later recovered and took a position by means of which she helped support the family. Then comes the girl of our story. This girl was always very healthy. Her mother had always been very much occupied with the two sick girls and with her husband, and did not have much time for this girl whom we shall call Anne. There was a younger boy, also brilliant and sick, and as a result Anne found herself crushed, so to speak, between two very beloved children. She was a good child, but felt that she was not as much liked as the others. She complained of being slighted and of feeling suppressed.

In school, however, Anne did good work. She was the best pupil. On account of her excellence in her studies the teacher recommended that she continue her education, and when she was only thirteen and a half she went to high school. Here she found a new teacher, who did not like her. Perhaps in the beginning she was not a good pupil, but any way with the lack of appreciation she grew worse. She had not been a problem child as long as she was appreciated by her old teacher. She had had good reports and had been well liked by her comrades. An individual psychologist could have seen even that something was wrong by looking at her friendships. She was always criticising her friends and always wanted to rule them. She wanted to be the center of attention and to be flattered, but never to be criticised.

Anne's goal was to be appreciated, to be favored and to be looked after. She found she could accomplish this only in school not at home. But at the new school she found appreciation blocked there, too. The teacher scolded her, insisted that she was not prepared, gave her bad reports, so that at last she became a truant and stayed away altogether for a few days. When she came back, things were worse than ever, and in the end the teacher proposed that she be expelled from school

Now expulsion from school accomplishes nothing. It is a confession on the part of the school and teacher that they cannot solve the problem. But if they cannot solve the problem they should call in others, who perhaps might be able to do something. Perhaps after talking with her parents arrangements might have been made to try another school. Perhaps there might have been another teacher who

115

would have understood Anne better. But her teacher did not reason that way; she reasoned, "If a child plays truant and is backward, she must be expelled." Such reasoning is a manifestation of private intelligence, not of common sense, and common sense is specially to be expected in a teacher.

We can guess what happened next. The girl lost her last hold in life and felt that everything was failing her. On account of being expelled from school, she lost even her slight modicum of appreciation at home. And so she ran away from both home and school. She disappeared for some days and nights. Finally it develops that she has had a love affair with a soldier.

We can easily understand her action. Her goal was to be appreciated, and up to this time she had been trained toward the useful side, but now she began her training on the useless side. This soldier in the beginning appreciated her and liked her. Later, however, the family received letters from her saying that she was pregnant and that she wanted to take poison.

This action of writing to her folks is in line with her character. She is always turning in the direction in which she expects to find appreciation and she keeps turning until she comes back home. She knows that her mother is in despair and that she will not therefore be scolded. Her family, she feels, will be only too glad to find her again.

In treating a case of this sort, identification the ability to place oneself sympathetically in the situation of a person is all-important. Here is an individual who wants to be appreciated and is pushing forward towards this one goal. If one were to identify oneself with such a person, one would ask himself, "What would I do?" Sex and age must be considered. We should always try to encourage such a person but encourage her towards the useful side. We should try to get her to the point where she would say, "Perhaps I should change my school, but I am not backward. Perhaps I have not trained enough perhaps I have not observed rightly perhaps I showed too much private intelligence at school and did not understand the teacher." If it is possible to lend courage, then a person will learn to train on the useful side. It is the lack of courage connected with an inferiority complex that ruins a person.

Let us put another person in the girl's place. A boy, for example, at her 'age might become a criminal. Such cases are often met with. If a boy loses courage in school, he is likely to drift away and become a member of a gang. Such behavior is easily understood. When he loses hope and courage, he will begin to be tardy, forge signatures to excuses, not do his homework, and look for places where he can play truant. In such places he finds companions who have gone the same way before, and now he becomes a member of a gang. He loses all interest in school, and he develops more and more a private understanding.

The inferiority complex is often connected with the idea that a person has no special abilities. The opinion is that some persons are gifted and others not. Such a view is itself an expression of an inferiority complex. According to Individual Psychology, "Everybody can accomplish everything," and it is a sign of an inferiority complex when a boy or girl despairs of following this maxim and feels unable to accomplish his goal on the useful side of life.

As part of the inferiority complex we have the belief in inherited characteristics. If this belief were really true if success were completely dependent upon innate ability then the psychologist could accomplish nothing. Actually, however, success is dependent on courage, and the task of the psychologist is to transform the feeling of despair into a feeling of hopefulness which rallies energies for the performance of useful work.

We see sometimes a youth of sixteen expelled from school and committing suicide out of despair. The suicide is a sort of revenge an accusation against society. It is the youth's way of affirming himself, via private intelligence, instead of via common sense. All that is necessary in such a situation is to win over the boy and to give him courage to take the useful path.

We can take many other examples. Consider a case of a girl, eleven years old, who was not liked at home. All the other children were preferred, and she felt she was not wanted. She became peevish, pugnacious and disobedient. It is a case that we can analyze quite simply. The girl felt she was not appreciated. In the beginning she tried to struggle, but then she lost hope. One day she began to steal. For the individual psychologist when a child steals, it is not so much a crime as a case of a movement of the child to enrich herself. It is not possible to enrich oneself unless one feels deprived. Her stealing was thus the result of her lack of affection at home and of her feeling of hopelessness. We will always notice that children begin to steal when they feel deprived. Such a feeling may not express the truth, but it is nonetheless the psychological cause for their action.

Another case is that of an eight-year-old boy au illegitimate, ugly child who was living with foster parents. These foster parents did not take good care of him and did not restrain him. Sometimes the mother gave him candy, and this was a bright spot in his life. When candy was scarce the poor boy suffered terribly. His mother had married an old man and had one child by him, and this child was the old man's only pleasure. He pampered her continually. The only reason the pair kept the boy was in order not to have to pay any money for his maintenance outside. When the old man came home he would bring candy for the little girl, but none for the boy. As a result the boy began to steal candy. He stole because he felt deprived, and wanted to enrich himself. The father beat him for stealing, but he kept on. One might think that the boy showed courage in that he kept on in spite of the beatings, but this is not true. He always had the hope of escaping detection.

This is a case of a hated child never experiencing what it means to be a fellow-man. We have to win him. We must give him the opportunity of living as a fellow-man. When he learns to identify and to place himself in others' positions he will understand how his stepfather feels when he sees him stealing and how the little girl feels when she discovers her candy gone. We see here again how lack of social feeling, lack of understanding and lack of courage go together to form an inferiority complex in this case the inferiority complex of a hated child.

CHAPTER ELEVEN

LOVE AND MARRIAGE

THE right preparation for love and marriage is first of all to be a fellow-man and to be socially adjusted. Along with this general preparation should be put a certain training of the instinct of sex from early childhood down to adult maturity a training that has in view the normal satisfaction of the instinct in marriage and a family. All the abilities, disabilities and inclinations for love and marriage can be found in the prototype formed in the first years of life. By observing the traits in the prototype we are able to put our finger on the difficulties that appear later in adult life.

The problems that we meet in love and marriage are of the same character as the general social problems. There are the same difficulties and the same tasks, and it is a mistake to regard love and marriage as a paradise in which all things happen according to one's desires. There are tasks throughout, and these tasks must be accomplished with the interests of the other person always in mind.

More than the ordinary problems of social adjustment, the love and marriage situation requires an exceptional sympathy, an exceptional ability to identify oneself with the other person. If few persons are properly prepared nowadays for family life it is that they have never learned to see with the eyes, hear with the ears, and feel with the heart of another.

Much of our discussion in the previous chapters has centered on the type of child who grows up interested only in himself and not in others. Such a type cannot be expected to change his character overnight with the maturing of the physical sex instinct. He will be unprepared for love and marriage in the same way that he is unprepared for social life.

Social interest is a slow growth. Only those persons who are really trained in the direction of social interest from their first childhood and who are always striving on the useful side of life will actually have social feeling. For this reason it is not particularly difficult to recognize whether a person is really well prepared for life with the other sex or not.

We need only to remember what we have observed with regard to the useful side of life. A person on that side of life is courageous and has confidence in himself. He faces the problems of life and goes on to find solutions. He has comrades, friends and gets along with his neighbors. A person who does not have these traits is not to be trusted and is not to be regarded as prepared for love and marriage. On the other hand we may conclude that a person is probably ready for marriage if he has an occupation and is progressing in it. We judge by a small sign, but the sign is very significant in that it indicates whether or not a person has social interest.

An understanding of the nature of social interest shows us that the problems of love and marriage can be solved satisfactorily only on the basis of entire equality. This fundamental giveand-take is the important thing; whether one partner esteems the other is not very significant. Love by itself does not settle things, for there are all kinds of love. It is only when there is a proper foundation of equality that love will take the right course and make marriage a success.

If either the man or the woman wishes to be a conqueror after marriage, the results are likely to be fatal. Looking forward to marriage with such a view in mind is not the right preparation, and the events after marriage are likely to prove it. It is not possible to be a conqueror in a situation in which there is no place for a conqueror. The marriage situation calls for an interest in the other person and an ability to put oneself in the other's place.

We turn now to the special preparation necessary for marriage. This involves, as we have seen, the training of the social feeling in connection with the instinct of sexual attraction. As a matter of fact we know that everyone creates in his own mind from childhood days on an ideal of a person of the other sex. In the case of a boy it is very probable that the mother plays the role of the ideal, and that the boy will always look for a similar type of woman to marry. Sometimes there may be a state of unhappy tension between the boy and his mother, in which case he will probably look for the opposite type of girl. So close is the correspondence between the child's relation with his mother and the type of woman he afterwards marries that we can observe it in such little details as eyes, figure, color of hair, etc.

We know, too, that if the mother is domineering and suppresses the boy, he will not want to go on courageously when the time comes for love and marriage. For in such a case his sexual ideal is likely to be a weak, obedient type of girl. Or, if he is a pugnacious type, he will also fight with his wife after marriage and want to dominate her.

We can see how all the indications manifested in childhood are emphasized and increased when a person faces the problem of love. We can imagine how a person suffering from an inferiority complex will behave in sexual matters. Perhaps because he feels weak and inferior he will express the feeling by always wanting to be supported by other persons. Often such a type has an ideal which is motherly in character. Or sometimes, by way of compensation for his in feriority, he may take the opposite direction in love and become arrogant, impudent and aggressive. Then, too, if he has not very much courage he will feel restricted in his choice. He may possibly select a pugnacious girl, finding it more honorable to be the conqueror in a severe battle.

Neither sex can act successfully in this way. It seems silly and ridiculous to have the sexual relationship exploited for the satisfaction of an inferiority or superiority complex, and yet this happens very frequently. If we look closely we see that the mate that many a person seeks is really a victim. Such persons do not understand that the sex relationship cannot be exploited for such an end. For if one person seeks to be a conqueror, the other will want

122

to be a conqueror also. As a result life in common becomes impossible.

The idea of satisfying one's complexes illuminates certain peculiarities in the choice of a partner which are otherwise difficult to understand. It tells us why some persons choose weak, sick, or old persons: they choose them because they believe things will be easier for them. Sometimes they look for a married person: here it is a case of never wanting to reach a solution of a problem. Sometimes we find people falling in love with two men or two women at the same time, because, as we have already explained, "two girls are less than one."

We have seen how a person who suffers from an inferiority complex changes his occupation, refuses to face problems, and never finishes tilings. When confronted with the problem of love he acts in a similar fashion. Falling in love with a married person or with two persons at once is a way of satisfying his habitual tendency. There are other ways, too, as for instance, overlong engagements, or even perpetual courtships, which are never consummated into marriage.

Spoiled children show up in marriage true to type. They want to be pampered by their marital partners. Such a state of affairs may exist without danger in the early stages of courtship or in the first years of marriage, but later it will bring about a complicated situation. We can imagine what happens when two such pampered persons marry. Both want to be pampered, and neither of them wants to play the pamperer. It is as if they stood before one another expecting something which neither gives. Both have the feeling that they are not understood.

We can understand what happens when a person feels himself misunderstood and his activity curtailed. He feels inferior and wants to escape. Such feelings are especially bad in marriage, particularly if a sense of extreme hopelessness arises. When this happens revenge begins to creep in. One person wants to disturb the life of the other person. The most common way to do this is to be unfaithful. Infidelity is always a revenge. True, persons who are unfaithful always justify themselves by speaking of love and sentiments, but we know the value of feelings and sentiments. Feelings always agree with the goal of superiority, and should not be regarded as arguments.

As an illustration we may take the case of a certain pampered woman. She married a man who had always felt himself curtailed by his other brother. We can see how this man was attracted by the mildness and sweetness of this only girl, who in turn expected always to be appreciated and preferred. The marriage was quite happy until a child came. And then we can predict what happened. The wife wanted to be the center of attention but was afraid that the child might step into that position. And so she was not very happy to have given birth to the child. The husband, on the other hand, also wanted to be preferred and was afraid that the child would usurp his place. As a result both husband and wife became suspicious. They did not perhaps neglect the child and were quite good parents, but they were always expecting that their love for each other would decrease. Such a suspicion is dangerous, because if one starts to measure every word, every action, movement and expression, it is easy to find, or to appear to find, a decrease in affection. Both parties found it. As it happened the husband went on a holiday, travelled to Paris and enjoyed himself while his wife recuperated from childbirth and looked after the infant. The husband wrote gay letters from Paris, telling his wife what good a time he was having, how he met all sorts of people, etc. The wife began to feel herself forgotten. And so she was not as happy as before, but became quite depressed and soon began to suffer from agorophobia. She could not go out alone any more. When her husband returned he always had to accompany her. On the surface at least, it would seem that she had attained her goal, and that she was now the center of attention. But nonetheless it was not the right satisfaction, for she had the feeling that if her agorophobia disappeared, her husband would disappear, too. Hence she continued to have agorophobia.

During this illness she found a doctor who gave her much attention. While under his care she felt much better. What feelings of friendship she had were all directed towards him. But when the doctor saw that the patient was better, he left her. She wrote him a nice letter thanking him for all he had done for her, but he did not answer. From this time on the illness became worse.

At this time she began to have ideas and fancies about liaisons with other men in order to revenge herself against her husband. However, she was protected by her agorophobia, inasmuch as she could not go out alone but had always to be accompanied by her husband. And thus she could not succeed in being unfaithful.

We see so many mistakes made in marriage that the question inevitably arises, "Is all this necessary?" We know that these mistakes were begun in childhood, and we know, too, that it is possible to change mistaken styles of life by recognizing and discovering the prototype traits. One wonders, therefore, whether it would not be possible to establish advisory councils which could untangle the mistakes of matrimony by the methods of Individual Psychology. Such councils would be composed of trained persons who would understand how all the events in individuals' lives cohere and hang together, and who would have the power of sympathetic identification with the persons seeking advice.

Such councils would not say: "You cannot agree you quarrel continuously you should get a divorce." For what use is a divorce? What happens after a divorce? As a rule the divorced persons want to marry again and continue the same style of life as before. We sometimes see persons who have been divorced time and again, and still they remarry. They simply repeat their mistakes. Such persons might ask this advisory council whether their proposed marriage or love relation had in it any possibility of success. Or they might consult it before obtaining a divorce.

There are a number of little mistakes which begin in childhood and which do not seem important until marriage. Thus some persons always think they will be disappointed. There are children who are

125

never happy and who are constantly in fear of being disappointed. These children either feel that they have been displaced in affection and that another will be preferred, or else an early difficulty which they experienced has made them superstitiously afraid that the tragedy may recur again. We can easily see that this fear of disappointment will create jealousies and suspicions in married life.

Among women there is a particular difficulty in that they feel they are only toys for men to play with, and that men are always unfaithful. With such an idea it is easy to see that marriage will not be happy. Happiness is impossible if one party has the fixed idea that the other is likely to be unfaithful.

From the way in which people always seek advice on love and marriage, one would judge that it is generally regarded as the most important question of life. From the point of view of Individual Psychology, however, it is not the most important question, although its importance is not to be undervalued. For Individual Psychology no one question in life is more important than another. If persons accentuate the question of love and marriage and give it a paramount importance they lose the harmony of life.

Perhaps the reason why this question is given such undue importance in the minds of people is that, unlike other questions, this is a topic on which we do not get any regular instruction. Recollect what we have said about the three great questions of life. Now as regards the first, the social question, which involves our behavior with others, we are taught from the first day of our life how to act in the company of others. We learn these things quite early. We likewise have a regular course of training for our occupations. We have masters to instruct us in these arts, and we have also books which tell us what to do. But where are the books that tell us how to prepare for love and marriage? To be sure there are a great many which deal with love and marriage. All literature deals with love stories, but we will find few books which deal with happy marriages. Because our culture is so tied up with literature everybody has his attention fixed on portraits of men and women who are always in difficulties, No wonder people feel cautious and overcautious about marriage.

This has been the practice of mankind from the beginning. If we look at the Bible we will find there the story that woman began all the trouble, and that ever since then men and women have always experienced great dangers in their love life. Our education is certainly too strict in the direction it follows. Instead of preparing boys and girls as if for sin, it would be much wiser to train the girls better in the feminine and the boys in the masculine role of marriage but train them both in such way that they would feel equal.

The fact that women now feel inferior proves that, in this particular, our culture has failed. If the reader is not convinced of this, let him look at the strivings of women. He will find that they usually want to overcome others and that often they develop and train more than is necessary. They are also more self -centered than men. In the future women must be taught to develop more social interest and not always to seek benefit for themselves without regard for others. But in order to do this, we must first banish the superstition regarding the privileges of men.

Let us take an instance to show how poorly prepared for marriage some people are. A young man was dancing at a ball with a pretty young girl whom he was engaged to marry. He happened to drop his glasses, and to the utter amazement of the spectators he almost knocked the young lady down in order to pick them up. When a friend asked him, "What were you doing ?" he replied, "I could not let her break my glasses." We can see that this young man was not prepared for marriage. And indeed the girl did not marry him.

Later in life he came to the doctor and said he was suffering from melancholia, as is often the case with persons who are too much interested in themselves.

There are a thousand signs by which one can understand whether or not a person is prepared for marriage. Thus one should not trust a person in love who comes late for an appointment without an adequate excuse. Such action shows a hesitating attitude. It is a sign of lack of preparation for the problems of life.

It is also a sign of lack of preparation if one member of a couple always wants to educate the other or always wants to criticise. Also to be sensitive is a bad sign, since it is an indication of an inferiority complex. The person who has no friends and does not mix well in society is not well prepared for marital life. Delay in choosing an occupation is also not a good sign. A pessimistic person is ill-fitted, doubtless because pessimism betrays a lack of courage to face situations.

Despite this list of undesirables it should not be so difficult to choose the right person, or rather to choose a person along the right lines. We cannot expect to find the ideal person. And indeed if we see someone looking for an ideal person for marriage and never finding him or her, we may be sure that such a person is suffering from a hesitating attitude. Such a person does not want to go on at all.

There is an old German method for finding out whether a couple is prepared for marriage. It is the custom in rural districts to give the couple a double-handled saw, each person to hold one end, and then have them saw the trunk of a tree while all the relatives stand around and watch. Now sawing a tree is a task for two persons. Each one has to be interested in what the other is doing and harmonize his strokes with his. This method is thus considered a good test of fitness for marriage.

In conclusion we reiterate our statement that the questions of love and marriage can be solved only by socially adjusted persons. The mistakes in the majority of cases are due to lack of social interest, and these mistakes can be obviated only if the persons change. Marriage is a task for two persons. Now it is a fact that we are educated either for tasks that can be performed by one person alone or else by twenty persons never for a task for two persons. But despite our lack of education the marriage task can be handled properly if the two persons recognize the mistakes in their character and approach things in a spirit of equality.

It is almost needless to add that the highest form of marriage is monogamy. There are many persons who claim on pseudo-scientific grounds that polygamy is better adapted to the nature of human beings. This conclusion cannot be accepted, and the reason it cannot be accepted is that in our culture love and marriage are social tasks. We do not marry for our private good only, but indirectly for the social good. In the last analysis marriage is for the sake of the race.

CHAPTER TWELVE

SEXUALITY AND SEX PROBLEMS

WE discussed in the preceding chapter the normal problems of love and marriage. We turn now to a more specific phase of the same general question the problems of sexuality and their bearing upon real or fancied abnormalities. We have already seen that in the questions of love life, most persons are less well prepared and less well trained than for the other questions of life. This conclusion applies with even greater force to the topic of sex. In questions of sexuality it is extraordinary how many superstitions must be wiped out.

The most common superstition is that of inherited characteristics the belief that there are degrees of sexuality which are inherited and which cannot be changed. We know how easily questions of inheritance can be used as excuses or subterfuges, and how these subterfuges can hinder improvement. It is necessary therefore to clarify some of the opinions that are advanced on behalf of science. These views are taken too seriously by the average layman, who do not realize that these authors give only the results and do not discuss either the degree of inhibition possible or the artificial stimulation of the sex instinct which is responsible for the results.

Sexuality exists very early in life. Every nurse or parent who observes carefully can find in the first days after the birth of a child that there are certain sexual irritations and movements. However, this display of sexuality is much more dependent upon environment than one might expect. And so when a child begins to express himself in this way, the parents should find ways to distract him. Often they use means which do not produce the right type of distraction, and sometimes the right means are not available.

If a child does not at an early stage find the correct functions, he may naturally develop a greater desire for sexual movements.

These things happen, we have seen, as regards other organs of the body, and the sex organs are no exception. But if one begins early it is possible to train the child correctly.

In general it may be said that some sex expression in childhood is quite normal, and we should not therefore be terrified by the sight of sexual movements in a child. After all, the goal of each sex is to be eventually joined to the other. Our policy should therefore be one of watchful waiting. We must stand by and see that sexual expression does not develop in the wrong direction.

There is a tendency to attribute to inherited deficiency what is really the result of self -training during childhood. Sometimes this very act of training is regarded as an inherited characteristic. Thus if a child happens to be more interested in his own sex than in the opposite sex, this is considered an inherited disability. But we know that this disability is something which he develops from day to day. Sometimes a child or adult shows signs of sex perversion; and here again many persons believe the perversion to be inherited. But if this is the case, why does such a person train himself? Why does he dream and rehearse his actions?

Certain persons stop this training at a certain time, and this fact can be explained along the lines of Individual Psychology. There are, for example, those who fear defeat. They have an inferiority complex. Or they may train so far that the result is a superiority complex, and in a case of this kind we will note an exaggerated movement which looks like overstressed sexuality. Such persons may possess greater sexual power.

This type of striving may he specially stimulated by the environment. We know how pictures, books, movies, or certain social contacts tend to over-stress this sex drive. In our time one may say that everything tends to develop an exaggerated interest in sex. One need not depreciate the great importance of these organic drives and of the part they play in love, marriage and the procreation of mankind, in order to assert that sex is over-emphasized at the present time.

131

It is the exaggeration of sex tendencies that is most to be guarded against by the parents who watch their children. Thus too often a mother pays too much attention to the first sexual movements in childhood and thereby tends to make the child overvalue their significance. She is perhaps terrified and is always occupied with such a child, always talking to him about these matters and punishing him. Now we know that many children like to be the center of attention, and hence it is frequently the case that a child continues in his habits precisely because he is scolded for them. It is better not to over-value the subject with a child, but to treat the matter as of one of the ordinary difficulties. If one does not show children that one is impressed by these matters, one will have a much easier time.

Sometimes there are traditions back of the child which incline him in a certain direction. It may be that the mother is not only affectionate, but expresses her affection in kisses, embraces, etc. Such things should not be overdone, although many mothers insist that they cannot resist doing them. Such actions, however, are not an example of motherly love. It is treating the child like an enemy rather than like a mother's child. A pampered child does not develop well sexually.

In this connection it may be pointed out that many doctors and psychologists believe that the development of sexuality is the basis for the development of the whole mind and psyche, as well as for all the physical movements. In the view of the present writer this is not true, inasmuch as the whole form and development of sexuality is dependent upon the personality the style of life and the prototype.

Thus, for example, if we know that a child expresses his sexuality in a certain way, or that another child suppresses it, we may guess what will happen to both of them in their adult life. If we know that the child always wants to be the center of attention and to conquer, then he will also develop his sexuality so as to conquer and be the center of attention.

Many persons believe that they are superior and dominant when they express their sex instinct polygamously. They therefore have sex relations with many, and it is easy to see that they deliberately overstress their sexual desires and attitudes for psychological reasons. They think that thereby they will be conquerors. This is an illusion, of course, but it serves as a compensation for an inferiority complex.

It is the inferiority complex which is the core of sexual abnormalities. A person who suffers from an inferiority complex is always looking for the easiest way out. Sometimes he finds this easiest way by excluding most of life and exaggerating his sexual life.

In children we find this tendency very often. Generally we find it among children who want to occupy others. They occupy their parents and teachers by creating difficulties and thus following out their striving on the useless side of life. Later in life they will occupy others with their tendencies and want to be superior in that way. Such children grow up confusing their sexual desire with the desire for conquest and superiority. Sometimes, in the course of their exclusion of part of the possibilities and problems of life, they may exclude the whole of the other sex and train homosexually. It is significant that among perverted persons an over-stressed sexuality is often to be found. They in fact exaggerate their tendency to be perverted as an insurance against having to face the problem of normal sex life which they wish to avoid.

We can understand all this only if we understand their style of life. We have here persons who want to have much attention paid to them and who yet believe themselves incapable of interesting the other sex sufficiently. They have an inferiority complex in regard to the other sex which may be traced back to childhood. For instance, if they found the behavior of the girls in the family and the behavior of the mother more attractive than their own, they got the feeling that they will never have the power to interest women. They may admire the opposite sex so much that they begin to imitate the

133

members of that sex. Thus we see men who appear like girls, and likewise girls who appear like men.

There is the case of a man accused of sadism and of actions against children which well illustrates the formation of the tendencies we have discussed. Inquiring into his development, we learn that he had a ruling and dominating mother who was always criticising him. Despite this he developed into a good and intelligent pupil at school. But his mother was never satisfied with his success. For this reason he wanted to exclude his mother from his family affections. He was not interested in her, but he occupied himself with his father and was greatly attached to him. We can see how such a child might get the idea that women are severe and hypercritical and that contact with them is not to be made with pleasure but only in case of great necessity. In this way he came to exclude the other sex. This person, moreover, was of a familiar type who is always sexually irritated when afraid. Suffering from anxiety and being thus irritated, this type constantly looks for situations where he will not be afraid. Later in life he might like to punish or torture himself, or see a child tortured, or even fancy himself or another tortured. And because he is of the type described, he will have sexual irritation and satisfactions in the course of this real or imaginary tortures.

The case of this man indicates the result of wrong training. The man never understood the interconnection of his habits, or if he did, he only saw it when it was too late. Of course it is very difficult to start to train a person properly at the age of 25 or 30. The right time is early childhood.

But in childhood matters are complicated by the psychological relations with the parents. It is curious to see how bad sexual training results as an incident in the psychological conflict of child and parent. A fighting child, especially in the period of adolescence, may abuse sexuality with the deliberate intention of hurting the parents. Boys and girls have been known to have sex relations just after a fight with their parents. Children take these means of revenging themselves on their parents particularly when they see

134

that they are sensitive in this regard. A fighting child will almost invariably take this point of attack.

The only way such tactics can be avoided is to make each child responsible for himself, so that he should not believe that it is the parents' interest alone which is at stake, but his own as well.

Besides the influence of childhood environment as reflected in the style of life, political and economic conditions in a country have their influence on sexuality. These conditions give rise to a social style which is very contagious. After the Russo-Japanese war and the collapse of the first revolution in Russia, when all the people had lost their hope and confidence, there was a great movement of sexuality known as Saninism. All the adults and adolescents were caught up in this movement. One finds a similar exaggeration of sexuality during revolution, and it is of course notorious that in war time there is a great recourse to sexual sensuality because life seems worthless.

It is curious to note that the police understand this use of sexuality as a psychological release. In Europe at least, whenever any crime is committed, the police look usually in the houses of prostitutes. There they find the murderer or other criminal that they are looking for. The criminal is there because after committing a crime he feels over-strained and looks for relief. He wants to convince himself of his strength and to prove that he is still a powerful being and not a lost soul.

A certain Frenchman has remarked that man is the only animal that eats when he is not hungry, drinks when he is not thirsty and has sex relations at all times. The over-indulgence of the sex instinct is really quite on a par with the overindulgence of other appetites. Now when any appetite is over-indulged and any interest is overdeveloped, the harmony of life is interfered with. Psychological annals are full of cases of persons who develop interests or appetites to the point where they become a compulsion with them. The cases of misers who overstress the importance of money are familiar to the common man. But there are also the cases of persons

135

who think cleanliness all important. They put washing ahead of all other activities and at times they wash the whole day and half the night. Then there are persons who insist on the paramount importance of eating. They eat all day long, are interested only in eatables, and talk about nothing but eating.

The cases of sexual excess are precisely similar. They lead to an unbalancing of the entire harmony of activity. Inevitably they drag the whole style of life to the useless side.

In the proper training of the sex instinct the sexual drives should be harnessed to a useful goal in which the whole of our activities are expressed. If the goal is properly chosen neither sexuality nor any other expression of life will be overstressed.

On the other hand while all appetites and interests have to be controlled and harmonized, there is danger in complete suppression. Just as in the matter of food, when a person diets to the extreme, his mind and body suffer, so, too, in the matter of sex complete abstinence is undesirable.

What this statement implies is that in a normal style of life sex will find its proper expression. It does not mean that we can overcome neuroses, which are the marks of an unbalanced style of life, merely by free sex expression. The belief, so much propagated, that a suppressed libido is the cause of a neurosis is untrue. Rather it is the other way around: neurotic persons do not find their proper sex expression.

One meets persons who have been advised to give more free expression to their sex instincts and who have followed that advice, only to make their condition worse. The reason things work out that way is that such persons fail to harness their sexual life with a socially useful goal, which alone can change their neurotic condition. The expressions of sex instinct by itself does not cure the neurosis, for the neurosis is a disease in the style of life, if we may use the term, and it can be cured only by ministering to the style of life.

136

For the individual psychologist all this is so clear that he does not hesitate to fall back on happy marriage as the only satisfactory solution for sex troubles. A neurotic does not look with favor on such a solution, because a neurotic is always a coward and not well prepared for social life. Similarly all persons who overstress sexuality, talk of polygamy, and companionate or trial marriage are trying to escape the social solution of the sex problem. They have no patience for solving the problem of social adjustment on the basis of mutual interest between husband and wife and dream of escape through some new formula. The most difficult road, however, is sometimes the most direct.

CHAPTER THIRTEEN

CONCLUSION

IT is time now to conclude the results of our survey. The method of Individual Psychology we have no hesitation in confessing it begins and ends with the problem of inferiority.

Inferiority, we have seen, is the basis for human striving and success. On the other hand the sense of inferiority is the basis for all our problems of psychological maladjustment. When the individual does not find a proper concrete goal of superiority, an inferiority 'complex results. The inferiority complex leads to a desire for escape and this desire for escape is expressed in a superiority complex, which is nothing more than a goal on the useless and vain side of life offering the satisfaction of false success.

This is the dynamic mechanism of psychological life. More concretely, we know that the mistakes in the functioning of the psyche are more harmful at certain times than at others. We know that the style of life is crystallized in tendencies formed in childhood in the prototype that develops at the age of four or five. And this being so, the whole burden of the guidance of our psychological life rests on proper childhood guidance.

As regards childhood guidance we have shown that the principal aim should be the cultivation of proper social interests in terms of which useful and healthy goals can be crystallized. It is only by training children to fit in with the social scheme that the universal sense of inferiority is harnessed properly and is prevented from engendering either an inferiority or superiority complex.

Social adjustment is the obverse face of the problem of inferiority. It is because the individual man is inferior and weak that we find human beings living in society. Social interest and social cooperation are therefore the salvation of the individual.